"If I am because I am I, and you are because you are you, then I am and you are. But If I am I because you are you and you are you because I am I, Then I am not and you are not."
                                                                                                                     -Gitte Lassen

"One day in retrospect the years of struggle will strike you as the most beautiful."
                                                                                                                     -Sigmund Freud

"Healing doesn't mean the damage never existed. It means the damage no longer controls our lives."
                                                                                                                     -Akshay Dubey

"Letting go doesn't mean that you don't care about someone anymore. It's just realizing that the only person you really have control over is yourself."
                                                                                                                     -Deborah Reber

Breaking Codependency

DR. LESLY DEVEREAUX

HARPERROBINS PUBLISHERS
PISCATAWAY

HarperRobins Publishers
Piscataway New Jersey 08854

Breaking Codependency: How to Navigate the Traps That Sabotage Your Life

Library of Congress Library of Congress Cataloging-in-Publication Data:

ISBN-978-0-9913276-0-7

Author's Note: As an independent contractor and writer, I have relied on personal experience, research, conclusions and opinions to write this book. Although I have quoted expert opinions as resources, this book does not necessarily reflect any viewpoint or opinions except my own. Neither the book nor I am affiliated with, represent, or work for any organization or treatment program. This information is not intended to be used as a medical diagnosis or a prescription for any medical, physical or mental ailments. Anyone seeking medical advice should personally meet with a qualified health practitioner. Names and certain details have been changed to ensure privacy and anonymity, but all stories in here are true; none are fictionalized or composites.

Editor's Note: This publication is not intended as a substitute for advices of health care professionals. The Twelve Steps are reprinted with the permission of Alcoholics Anonymous World Services, Inc. Permission to reprint does not mean that Alcoholics Anonymous has reviewed or approved the contents of this publication, or that AA agrees with the expressed views herein. AA is a program of recovery from alcoholism. Use of the Twelve Steps in connection with the programs and activities that are patterned after AA, but that address other problems, does not imply otherwise.

Printed and bound in the United States of America.

Breaking
Codependency

To My Husband
who weathered a major storm for the sake of our vows.
My heart delights in the true blessing that you embody.

CONTENTS

Foreword by
Barbara Rubel

I'll never forget the first time I met Lesly Devereaux. She and I were attending a business reinvention program hoping to develop new ideas about being resourceful women entrepreneurs. Years have passed since we shared those business concepts and have since implemented many of the strategies we set forth for ourselves. One of the goals Dr. Lesly as she is known, spoke of was to help women find purpose and joy in their lives. Little did I realize at the time, Dr. Lesly would take her own struggles with enabling, and write a book about how she broke the bonds of codependency and navigated the traps that sabotaged her own life.

Dr. Lesly has been extremely transparent with us as she shares her experience and her perspective on breaking codependency. What differentiates her book from other books on this topic is that you are brought into the life of the author as she navigates being incarcerated while reflecting on the enabling behaviors that put her there in the first place. Dr. Lesly's story shows us that we can break codependence at any point in time, and the sooner the better! Through the narrative of the author, a courageous speaker, coach and ordained minister, we are provided a valuable reference on how to break codependency. Its real value begins with the recommendations of how to stop enabling others.

If you picked up this book then you are either an enabler, know someone who is or you are trying to find out if you possess the characteristics. Additionally, this book will be a guide for mental health professionals, healthcare professionals, and victim/witness professionals who want to learn about this topic.

Your perspective and the way you define the term, enabling, is as unique as you are. Take for example, the victim/witness professional who acts unselfishly to help victims. She is extremely dedicated to her job, is especially close to the victims she serves and feels guilty about not being more involved. She becomes angry when victims do not do as she says, crosses several boundaries, and needs to be in control to avoid many of her personal problems. Her behaviors are causing her to feel stress, burnout, and compassion fatigue, and she is thinking of leaving victim services.

Other examples are:

- Offering babysitting services to a neighbor when you can hardly keep track of your own kids.
- Paying for a loved one's rent when you are barely making your own ends meet.
- Completing a co-worker's tasks and making excuses to your boss for their behavior when you are struggling to finish your own assignments.

Although some enabling behaviors are bothersome or exhausting, some actions can be deadly. I am speaking to you as a bereavement specialist, author of resources related to loss and burnout, and as a professional speaker on topics related to traumatic loss and compassion fatigue. Challenges in our personal and professional life can become complicated and overwhelming. All too often our relationships cause us stress, constant worry, and grief. I wish to emphasize the inevitable influence of enabling that can lead to a death and will illustrate this point through the following examples:

- A mother of an 18-year-old drug addict continues to give her daughter allowance even though she knows the money is being used to buy heroin. The daughter tells her mother that she will not attend college if her mother stops giving her money. The daughter overdoses after her high school graduation.
- A grandfather recognizes that his 24-year-old grandson has suicidal behavior and confronts his son and daughter-in-law about the red flags he is seeing. The parents tell him that they

are avoiding the issue out of fear that their son will become angry with them. Weeks pass and he continues to see his grandson spiraling out of control. Once again, he faces the issue that needs to be addressed with the grandson's parents. However, the parents continue to avoid it, noting that they fear their son's wrath if they bring up the topic. His grandson kills himself four days before his 25th birthday.

There are very few self-help resources that focus on enabling. While clinicians have created literature for professionals, less has been made available to lay readers seeking information about this topic. To me, the greatest contribution of this book lies in what it will do to also help you stop destructive behaviors. As you read this book, you will see how you should not:

- use enabling to feel important
- keep giving those you care about another chance to do the right thing
- avoid the problem with hopes that the person will be able to solve it without professional assistance

Try to fix individuals on your own and must either give the persons the skills to help themselves or reach out to professionals who are able to help them take responsibility for their actions.

Feel entitled as though individuals owe you because of all you have done for them.

I enthusiastically recommend that you read Dr. Lesly's book. Learn how to navigate the traps that sabotage your life and find joy in helping, not in enabling!

Barbara Rubel, MS, BCETS, CBS
Professional Speaker and Author of But I Didn't Say Goodbye
www.griefworkcenter.com

A note from the author

Writing can either be an exercise in frustration or it can be extremely cathartic. At the onset of my troubles in 2004, writing was the last thing on my mind. It was not until the Lord led me to seminary in 2005 that I began to truly enjoy the writing process. Differently than my legal career where writing was mostly persuasive and argumentative, the opportunity to write reflectively about my personal experience, in an open and candid way as the rule and not the exception, was a welcome relief.

Little did I know that reflective writing would force me to look at the person I had become or possibly had suppressed for most of my life. Theologically I was challenged to find God in my character and conduct. Today with my character and conduct intact, I am able to write this note to you confident that there are experiences that many of us will encounter in life that will either break us emotionally or cause us to emerge from it with a renewed sense of self and purpose borne out of pain. As I have said on many occasions, this challenge in my life has been a blessing and a curse. I choose to focus on the blessings that have come with learning who I was and in making a conscious choice in the person I want to be.

Failure is an interesting dilemma because if we go through life never having failed at anything, then the opportunity to learn, develop, grow and help others is greatly diminished. We have two choices that come with failure: either you fail flat, living with the guilt, hurt, shame and disappointment that it produces, causing you to feel that you can never get up; or you fail forward learning from the past but not holding on to it, instead choosing to take the lessons and use them to strengthen yourself.

I chose to fail forward. It is my prayer that when you fail you, too, will fail forward. There are some who are of the opinion that I should have kept my "experience of failure" to myself and simply walked quietly into the sunset. That is not the message I heard from God. The still small voice said there is power in your story to heal others who have been hurt and who need hope.

This book is for those who are looking for hope in life's challenges. If you can withhold judgment as you read the candid experience that I share in this book, then my prayer is that you will see that there truly is an upside to failure. Further I pray that you will learn something from my story by looking beyond my faults and carefully discerning your own needs.

While this is a story of my personal journey toward self-discovery, healing and redemption as I share my experience and encounter with the incarcerated women I call caged birds; it is also a source of helping you to deal with issues that may be causing you to spiral out of control. In order to protect and honor their privacy the names and some details of time and place have been altered.

Joyfully yours!

Dr. Lesly Devereaux, D.Min., J.D.
Abiding in Faith

"Success is not final, failure is not fatal:
it is the courage to continue that counts."
-Winston Churchill

Acknowledgements

FAMILY, THE UNBREAKABLE BOND

This book is dedicated to a community of family and friends who held me up when I wanted to fall. Les Devereaux my wonderful, supportive husband who had every reason to leave but understood the true meaning of the vows "for better or for worse," I love you. Shawn, Jaison and Isaiah, my wonderful sons, I love the young men that you have become. Thank you for loving me unconditionally. Mommy, you have always exuded the highest level of integrity, character and faith. My heart aches at what you endured but I am so proud of the strength that you demonstrated through it all. I love you, mommy. Candace, through your struggles you have emerged a true example of the power of God's transformative love. I know you did the right thing and I am proud to call you sister. I love you Aunt Betty. Thank you for praying.

COMMUNITY OF LOVE

There are so many people who prayed for me and with me during the darkest days of my life. Paulette, there are no words to express my gratitude. You stood by me when others did not. Thank you for being a true friend, mentor and the big sister that I always wanted. Cyril, I want to thank you for your sincere and unconditional friendship. Kelly, Lori, and Leroy, thank you for always stepping up on my behalf. Vesta and Cynthia, my prayer partners of twenty years, we truly have prayed each other through. Thank you for standing in the gap for your "PP." Geneva , Rev. Catina and the Mt. Zion AME New Brunswick Church family, thank you for the overabundance of love and support that you showed to my husband, son and me.

John Filimon, what God has brought together in our friendship no one can separate, thank you for the first edits of the book and the support that you continue to show. To my mentor and sister friend Barbara Rubel, you are amazing. Thank you for your advice, creativity and instruction during the writing process. I wish that I could name everyone who has been instrumental on this journey but I shall never forget. To all of you who watched my children, cooked meals for my family, lent me money and prayed, prayed, prayed, thank you. Your love, support and God's grace and mercy have made me whole.

CHEESE DOODLES (MY INCARCERATED SISTERS)

A journey of 1,000 miles begins with a single step.
Chinese Ancient Proverb

To my beloved incarcerated and formally incarcerated sisters who I affectionately call Cheese Doodles because of the color we were forced to wear. Thank you for protecting, loving and sharing your stories with me. I promised when I returned to society that I would not forget you. Although I do not know all of you personally I relate to your pain. I believe for you as I do for myself that brighter days are ahead. Do not let your past determine your future. There is glory in your story. Use it to forge ahead in a new direction. It is my prayer for you that in reading this book, you will put one foot in front of the other and walk into your wonderful destiny.

CONTRIBUTIONS

A special thanks to my editor Yvette Blair-Lavallais for your patience and for helping me clarify the best way to share my ideas. I also extend thanks to Nakia Laushaul for the fantastic layout design and typesetting, also to Vonda Howard for the book cover and to Cathryn Stanley for the magnificent book trailer.

Introduction

Do you suffer from codependency? Ask yourself these questions.

- Have you found yourself in an endless web of confusion and stress because of your need to come to the rescue of undeserving people that you love?
- Has helping the ones you love drained you and hurt them?
- Do you need help overcoming your desire to rescue people who continue on a course of self-destructive behavior?

If you answered yes to any of these questions you may be an enabler with the larger issue of codependency.

Does this sound like someone you know?

My definition of an enabler is a person who reinforces the negative behavior of another through a continuous course of rescue conduct. Enablers fuel self-destructive personalities in others. Enablers have a need to control and without regard to consequences; it is a dysfunctional approach on the part of the enabler which can, as in my case, become self-destructive, while allowing the enabled to sink further into bad behavior.

Codependency of which enabling is a major element does exist in families absent drug addiction. Melody Beattie, author of Codependent No More, popularized this phenomenon of codependency. She states that, "Codependency occurs when one person lets another person's behavior affect him or her, and who is obsessed with controlling that person's behavior." There is a strong nexus between codependency and enabling, which is mostly revealed in the characteristics of both. The enabler usually has un-prescribed issues of value and identity. Codependents behavioral problems amount to obsessive behavior, which results in a dysfunctional relationship between the codependent and others. Codependents have their own addiction, which is fueled by being needed. I use the words interchangeably because of my personal experience with perpetuating negative behavior in others and my un-prescribed condition of lack of self-worth.

I wrote this book because I was trapped in a cycle of codependency for many years. It was not until I fell into a deep dark pit called prison did I realize that it was time to make a change in how I cared for the people closest to me.

I never considered prison would ever be a part of my life. I was a prosecutor employed by the Essex County Prosecutor's Office. I prosecuted and won many cases. I had helped send people to prison. As a public defender, I defended and counseled many people who were sentenced to prison. On this day, January 14, 2008, the day before Martin Luther King Jr.'s birthday, a man I admired, I had no answer. This was a day like no other.

"All rise," the court officer shouted. Everyone in the courtroom immediately stood out of respect for the judge. I had a flashback to my brief stint as the first African-American woman Municipal Court judge in Piscataway, New Jersey. The authoritative sound of the gavel signified a command by the judge in charge. I had slammed the gavel on numerous individuals and now it was about to be slammed on me.

It was my turn to speak prior to sentencing. My attorney stood first and outlined my life accomplishments, all of which seemed insignificant at the moment. "Your Honor, Lesly Devereaux stands before you a wife, mother, daughter, and sister. While she accepts full responsibility for her actions after being found guilty by trial, we ask you to consider the following: She has an eleven-year-old son who has never been separated from his mother; she has no prior record; she has led a life of service in the community and church -" blah, blah, blah. That is how it began to sound. My mind was elsewhere. I knew I would have to speak, but I felt a lump in my throat and my heart was beating so fast.

I had tried to write a statement prior to sentencing day, but I kept scratching out the words and starting over. As my attorney sat down, I stood up. "Your Honor, I would like to apologize to the citizens of New Jersey, the employees of the Commerce Commission, my husband, children, mom, and sister for all that has happened. I accept responsibility for my actions and I am prepared to accept the consequences. I took my seat and waited. It was now Judge Bielamowicz's turn. "Will the defendant please rise?" I stood while she ripped into me, but the only thing I heard was: "I hereby sentence you to six-and-a-half years. You are now under the custody of the Department of Corrections."

What! This was only six months short of what the prosecutors had requested. We had hoped for probation but expected five years. There was a loud gasp in the courtroom. I do not think anyone expected the judge to give me so much time. I turned to my husband and friends, who were seated behind me, and said, "I'm all right. I am fine." I turned back around and stood tall, head held high, with an expressionless face. As the handcuffs were placed on my wrist and ankles I wondered if believing I could solve everyone's problems without thinking of the harm it could bring to them and me brought me to this day.

10 WAYS THIS BOOK WILL HELP YOU:

- Search your family tree to see if your actions are a result of learned behavior
- Identify and address your pain from the past
- Embrace your nurturing instincts as a woman with healthy boundaries
- Examine your conduct and change habits which challenge your moral compass
- Challenge yourself to say no even when you want to say yes
- Focus on self-care and not feel selfish
- Embrace the spiritual awakening which will take place
- Keep your head above the noise of fear, shame and rejection

- Detach from people that cause harm to your emotional stability
- Identify the characteristics of an enabler

How to use this book:

Breaking Codependency, which details a *lived* experience, is easy and fast to read. I don't want you to get caught up in academic, diagnostic, medical or psychological interpretations of codependency. I do not want you to expect a quick fix to an issue which you have probably struggled with for many years. However, if you want to truly work on navigating the codependency trap in order for transformation to occur I suggest that you take your time to read and reflect on each chapter.

Take advantage of the following:

- After each chapter there is a reflection exercise for you to participate in. There are a series of questions which challenge you to think about your life and behavior.
- Complete the exercises which are designed to help you delve deeper into your characteristics and behavior.
- As you read, I encourage you to highlight the sentences, thoughts and themes which you identify with.
- Keep a daily journal which includes challenges and triumphs. Be sure to include insights from the book which cause you to take action and control over your life.

Read this book with:

- Your book club. If you do not belong to a club start one with the women in your community or on a closed Facebook group.
- The women's ministry in your church.

- Your spouse who does not understand why you are doing so much for your family.
- The person you are enabling.
- Alone as you reflect on your life.

I invite you to journey with me as we navigate to a new beginning of healthy connectedness for you and the ones that you love. On to chapter one!

Chapter One
A Day Like No Other

"Nothing can dim the light that shines from within."
-Maya Angelou

I DID NOT sleep well last night. Restless, I finally dozed off around 2:00 a.m., only to awaken at 5:00 a.m. I did not want to get out of bed on this cold, dreary morning in January, but this was the one day that I could not sleep late. I got up and walked around the house, taking mental pictures of each detail of our home. I peeked in on my eleven-year-old son Isaiah and stared, unable to look away, and then I tip-toed in and placed a long, gentle kiss on his forehead while he slept. My other sons, Shawn and Jaison, were away at college. My husband, Les, was still asleep and I did not want to bother him, because I knew this would be an extra hard day for him. We had never been separated for any extended period of time since we were married. Today would be different.

I never liked the cold and always padded myself with extra layers of clothing before braving the weather. I did not want to leave my house, but I had to. I knew this day was coming and had tried to prepare myself emotionally and physically with prayer and counseling from friends in the ministry. I had gone to the gym every day to work out so that my body could withstand any possible health challenges. Over the past four years, I had lost about forty pounds. Usually, this is a thing most overweight women welcome. For me, the weight loss was a sign of stress. After all, how does one prepare for prison?

I never considered prison would ever be a part of my life. I was a prosecutor employed by the Essex County Prosecutor's Office. I prosecuted and won many cases. I had helped send people to prison. As a public defender, I defended and counseled many people who were sentenced to prison. On this day, January 14, 2008, the day before Martin Luther King Jr.'s birthday, a man I admired, I had no answer. This was a day like no other.

Normally, I dressed for court in business attire: black pants, white blouse, and business jacket. On the morning of January 14, I put on a gray sweat suit, long underwear and sneakers. As I walked out the door, I turned and took one last lingering look. While I did not know my fate—that was in the hands of Judge Bielamowicz—I was sure that I would not return to my home and family for a while.

Les got in the driver's seat and I settled into the front passenger seat. My sister Candace (I have called her Candy all of her life), was in the backseat. This was sentencing day for her, too. Neither Candace nor I were too concerned about her because the responsibility of what had occurred fell on me. Les was driving his usual careful speed, but today I thought to myself, why are we going so fast? On any given weekday the traffic flow on the New Jersey Turnpike at rush hour crawled. However, on this morning, the traffic was clear. We seemed to be moving faster than usual, faster than I wanted to go. The ride was quiet. We all seemed to be in our own thoughts. I kept looking out the window at the leafless trees, which in the spring turned green and in the fall were a beautiful mix of earth tone colors. In January, the scene was lifeless and barren. On the inside, I felt the same way - barren, lifeless - but looking forward to when this season in my life would change. I wondered: When will I see a highway, cars, my children, or my husband again? Is this day really happening?

FROM THE COURTHOUSE TO THE BIG HOUSE

Large, gothic, and in need of a facelift, the Mercer County Superior courthouse appeared on this day to be mammoth, bigger than normal. Looking up toward the top of the steps, I felt as if the doors seemed to be waiting for me, determined to swallow me up. I took my time climbing the twenty-five steps to the entrance. My walk was intentionally slow, a snail's pace, because I knew I would not be leaving the same way I entered. Today, Les, who is normally a fast walker, held my hand tightly and took each step with me. Over the past twelve years during our walks outside, Les and I always started out together, but he ended up leaving me behind because I could not keep up his pace. Today, and since this ordeal began, he has taken each step with me - mad, sad, or indifferent - and I am grateful. As we made our way to the entrance single file, I began taking off my jacket in order to go through the metal detector. The officer on duty, an older African-American man who has always spoken to me and never been nasty like some of the court officers, looked at me with sadness in his eyes. He quickly turned away as if not wanting others to see us make eye contact. The mood of the people in the hallway was quiet and tense. I knew there were a lot of people quietly rooting for me, and today I needed it.

To my surprise, I walked into a crowded courtroom filled with many of my supporters. Some of my enemies were present along with the media. My actions and politics had caused a ripple reaction in the New Jersey Commerce Commission and many people had been fired after I was indicted just because I hired them. While there was no accusation of improper hiring practices toward any of the individuals, it became guilt by association. I deeply regretted the hurt and disappointment I had caused and continued to struggle with the fact that many people had not forgiven me. The media had not been kind to my family or me. In their eyes I was just another corrupt public official who got caught. In reality, I never considered myself a public official or understood the great responsibility attached to the position. I practiced law for sixteen years prior to joining the Commerce Commission. I was and am still a devoted Christian who is part of an active congregation. I accepted the position at the request of my pastor. I thought it was okay to help family and friends like we did in church. As I reflect, I am not casting my ignorance as an excuse for poor judgment, which I admittedly used. I knew who I was, and it was not all bad. Had I made mistakes? Absolutely, and I was ready to face the music.

It took a while for Superior Court Judge Maryann K. Bielamowicz to enter the courtroom. While I was waiting one of the court officers came to me and led me to a hallway out of the presence of onlookers. He was trying to be kind without appearing weak. After all, he had a job to do, and that was to lock my butt up. The officer said, "You have to take all of your jewelry off, except your wedding ring." I knew from my conversation with people close to prison rules that I could wear a cheap gold band. So prior to the day of reckoning, I went to Wal-Mart and purchased a ten-dollar fake gold ring. When I got home, I swapped it for my three-and-a-half-carat wedding ring. My good friend Sara was standing with me in the hallway and she handed me a tiny New Testament Bible. I asked the court officer could I take it with me and he surprisingly said yes. I placed the bible in the pouch of my hoody sweat shirt and waited for the first opportunity to read God's word.

Everyone knew the judge was going to sentence me to jail, even though she could have given me probation. From the moment I walked into her courtroom, I knew Judge Bielamowicz did not care for me. Every ruling, even with her discretion, went against me, and she looked at me with cold eyes. She tried repeatedly to get my attorney to convince me to take a plea deal. A plea deal may have been an option, but the prosecutor wanted seven years of my life. My attorney presented other cases involving public officials with crimes more serious than mine – embezzlement, extortion, and bribery – and all were given probation. It was clear that I was being made an example because of my refusal to cooperate concerning other individuals. While I prayed that was not true, I was pretty sure that my sentence would be a term of imprisonment. The question was: How long? Obviously, the officer knew it, too, because he explained further that after the sentencing I would have to remain in the courtroom.

Upon my return to the courtroom, Judge Bielamowicz finally entered. "All rise," the court officer shouted. Everyone in the courtroom immediately stood out of respect for the judge. I had a flashback to my brief stint as the first African-American woman Municipal Court judge in Piscataway, New Jersey. The authoritative sound of the gavel signified a command by the judge in charge. I had slammed the gavel on numerous individuals and now it was about to be slammed on me.

The prosecutors had the opportunity to make a sentencing statement, and they let me have it. Reflecting on how they conducted themselves during the course of the trial, it bordered on personal hate. As a prosecutor, I knew my job was to seek justice. I thought about how I had treated defendants while in the position of prosecutor and it never had reached the level of rolling eyes, pointing fingers, smirks, and callous treatment of the defendant's family. Mutt and Jeff, as I called them, took it to a new level, acting like big bullies.

It was now my turn to speak prior to sentencing. My attorney stood first and outlined my life accomplishments, all of which seemed insignificant at the moment. "Your Honor, Lesly Devereaux stands before you a wife, mother, daughter, and sister. While she accepts full responsibility for her actions after being found guilty by trial, we ask you to consider the following: She has an eleven-year-old son who has never been separated from his mother; she has no prior record; she has led a life of service in the community and church" -blah, blah, blah. That is how it began to sound. My mind was elsewhere. I knew I would have to speak, but I felt a lump in my throat and my heart was beating so fast.

I had tried to write a statement prior to sentencing day, but I kept scratching out the words and starting over. As my attorney sat down, I stood up. "Your Honor, I would like to apologize to the citizens of New Jersey, the employees of the Commerce Commission, my husband, children, mom, and sister for all that has happened. I accept responsibility for my actions and I am prepared to accept the consequences. It is my hope and prayer that everyone can go on with their lives and now the prosecutors and media can focus on someone else. This is an unfortunate situation, but it does not define me." I took my seat.

I think I pissed the judge off with the last words. While she had been looking at me, suddenly she glanced down at a paper on her desk, scratched something out, and wrote something else. I am sure she increased my sentence at that moment. Her disdain for me was evident. It was now Judge Bielamowicz's turn. "Will the defendant please rise?" I stood while she ripped into me, but the only thing I heard was: "I hereby sentence you to six-and-a-half years. You are now under the custody of the Department of Corrections."

What! This was only six months short of what the prosecutors had requested. We had hoped for probation but expected five years. There was a loud gasp in the courtroom. I do not think anyone expected the judge to give me so much time. I turned to my husband and friends, who were seated behind me, and said, "I'm all right. I am fine." I turned back around and stood tall, head held high, with an expressionless face. Something came over me, and on the inside I was beaming with the light of peace. In the end, God had prepared me for this day, a day like no other.

I knew that my actions in 2004 were an act of care for my family but done in poor judgment. Even so, I did not anticipate the severity of the punishment. I was destined for exile, going to a place I did not want to go, nor a place that I ever imagined I could go. I asked myself, "How did I get here?" going to a place where nobody knows my name and nobody cares if they know my name. My name, Lesly Devereaux, had always been associated with achievement. I was a successful attorney and a woman who prided herself on helping others and doing her best in all circumstances. Now standing with my hands cuffed in the front, shackled at the waist and ankles, paraded through a hallway in front of news media, the public, my family, and friends, on my way to a foreign land with locked doors and bars for a time not certain, I thought, I am shackled but free, because to be free in Jesus is to be free indeed.

THE OTHER SIDE OF THE FENCE

My sister, Candace, was next for sentencing. Admittedly, she had problems in her past, but this time she really had not done anything wrong. She was accused of conspiracy to commit theft, misapplication of public property, and a host of other charges. The indictment was unsealed on December 7, 2004, which happened to be my 46th birthday. It originally named only me. A few days later, my attorney called and said my mother and sister had been indicted along with me. My mother was and is a woman of the highest integrity. She was guilty of nothing. It was my decision to offer her and my sister contract work, and I did. While the offering of a contract to a family member in and of itself is not a crime, the way I handled the situation was in question and I was willing to take the heat. My mom and sister stood with me praying that we would survive this terrible ordeal.

Candy did not stand trial in our case. We did not want to risk the jury convicting her on 16 counts which would result in her facing 22 years in prison so she agreed to a plea bargain. Believe it or not many people take pleas to crimes they did not commit rather than gamble on a jury verdict. Candy pled guilty to a third-degree charge of misapplication of funds. We all expected that she would get probation. The judge sentenced Candy to 365 days in the Mercer County Correctional Center. After the judge passed sentence, there was a gasp from the audience as tears rolled down my face. I knew that despite all of Candace's prior issues, this time my sister was really trying to legitimately work so that she could feed her children. I also thought about how my actions had placed my mom and her in this position. Neither she nor my mom had any notion that there was an issue with the contract work until I was informed of my possible indictment. For everything they endured, I am sorry.

The scene was straight out of a movie. It was time to begin our journey to the other side of the fence. The court was cleared, and as Les and my friends were leaving, I turned, kissed Les, and looked at everyone. "See you on the other side," I said. Candy became agitated and started talking loudly because of the thought of separation from her children. I told my sister, "Don't let them see you sweat. You are stronger than that." I knew that was what the prosecutors wanted. They lingered to see the handcuffs placed on our hands. It was behavior I did not understand. As a prosecutor, I never took pleasure in someone's defeat, but this crew was ecstatic.

We were both led to the jury box. There were four court officers surrounding us on all sides as if they were afraid we would run. I thought to myself, "Here we go." We were told to face the chair and put our knees on the seat. Our backs were now toward the officers. I could hear the shackles rattling, "Click, click." The shackles were placed on our ankles. We were then told to hop off the chair and turn around. Candy complained that the shackles were too tight. The officers did nothing. My instinct as one who looked out for my sister was to come to Candy's rescue, but I could not. A chain was wrapped around each of our waists and handcuffs were placed on our wrists. The shackles on our ankles connected us together. There is something to be said about healthy connectedness. Candy and I had never experienced it. I had never been in shackles or chains, so it took a minute for me to gain my balance. When we began to walk, we had to stay close and walk slowly. I was first in line. I had been first in many positive things in life. This was a first that I could have done without. We were officially a chain gang. Candace and I were paraded past the stares and silence of a crowd of people in the courthouse hallway.

I worried about my husband and how he would take seeing me shackled, escorted by court officers on my way to prison. I did not see Les as I walked through the hallway. I kept my eyes forward and my head held high. I am not sure if I would have been able to handle the disappointment in his eyes. The court officers were pretty decent. I think they were trying to be respectful. They knew the political circumstances surrounding my case and my background as an attorney, former judge, and chief of staff for the New Jersey Commerce Commission. I whispered to my sister to keep calm. We were in this thing now, and we had to see it through with dignity, as much as a shackled and chained convicted felon can do anything with dignity. I enabled Candy, I enabled my mother, and I enabled my brother. I destroyed myself, and this was the result—from the courthouse to the big house.

Soul Searching

I recall as a child watching films of criminals being carted off to prison. And now, here I was on my way to jail with my little sister. "Wake up, Lesly. It is only a dream," kept playing in my mind. Only it wasn't a dream.

As I always have been, I was worried about my sister and not myself. As I reflect on the times, trying to figure out where my need to take care of my siblings came from, days, months and years of soul searching occurred. I realized that as a child, a lot of responsibility was unintentionally shifted to me by my working mother who had no help from my emotionally absentee father. I use the word unintentional because with no other family support she had no choice. I was the middle child but acted like the oldest. I never gave my mother any problems.

My mother worked one full-time job and one part-time job

simultaneously. She also took classes to finish her college education. In trying to raise herself to a higher educational standard and provide for us she was challenged with time needed at home. Similar to many women leading single parent homes my mother was strong, devoted and determined to do what she had to in order to take care of her family. I had an older brother, but I was the oldest girl in the house. I exhibited an extreme amount of confidence at a young age. Because of my mother's faith in my abilities, I thought I could do anything. My sister, three years younger than I, was the baby, and she was treated that way. When my mother was at work, I was responsible for making sure my sister's homework was done and that the food was cooked, the kitchen was cleaned, and clothes were washed. If it got late and my mother was still out working her part time job I made sure my sister was in bed. My brother, Shawn, (whom my son is named for), who was starved for attention, exhibited at an early age behavior suggesting anger and lack of societal adjustment. My father, emotionally unavailable, addicted to drugs and unemployed is the person my brother looked to for approval.

Shouldering responsibility as a preteen shaped the way I acted and thought, and as I matured into adulthood, I realized its significance. Issues of control become a problem. I believed that I could fix anything and anyone without the help of others. As my sister and I matured and eventually started our adult lives, I was the one on the fast track to success. My sister reluctantly went to college. She did graduate. While she tried to keep many of her personal issues from me, I always knew when there was trouble in her life. When she was behind in her rent, I paid it. When she needed a place to live, I let her live with me. When she needed a job, I always tried to help her find one. I desperately wanted her to become an independent and self-sufficient person. In fact, I was doing exactly what I did not want to do, which showed through our constant arguments. I thought I could "fix" her by always coming to her rescue in times of trouble. I crippled my sister's independence by not allowing her to stand on her own two feet.

ENABLING A MAJOR ELEMENT OF CODEPENDENCY

This behavior, unfortunately, is one of the many characteristics of an enabler. My definition of an enabler is a person who reinforces the negative behavior of another through a continuous course of rescue conduct. Enablers fuel self-destructive personalities in others. Enablers have a need to control and without regard to consequences; it is a dysfunctional approach on the part of the enabler which can, as in my case, become self-destructive, while allowing the enabled to sink further into bad behavior.

Codependency of which enabling is a major element does exist in families absent drug addiction. Melody Beattie, author of Codependent No More, popularized this phenomenon of codependency. She states that, "Codependency occurs when one person lets another person's behavior affect him or her, and who is obsessed with controlling that person's behavior." There is a strong nexus between codependency and enabling, which is mostly revealed in the characteristics of both. The enabler usually has un-prescribed issues of value and identity. Codependents behavioral problems amount to obsessive behavior, which results in a dysfunctional relationship between the codependent and others. Codependents have their own addiction, which is fueled by being needed. I use the words interchangeably because of my personal experience with perpetuating negative behavior in others and my un-prescribed condition of lack of self-worth.

You may ask the question: Isn't everyone codependent or an enabler? My answer is no. The difference between an enabler and someone who is supportive of another person boils down to dysfunction. Your desire to help someone in need does not ultimately hurt them. If it does, it is a dysfunctional relationship. If the relationship is more important to you than yourself, it is a codependent relationship, which in fact enables another person.

THE BUBBLE

Through the stares and embarrassment, Candy and I walked on the chain gang escorted by the guards. Eventually, we made it through the crowd to an elevator where we were told to turn our entire body away from the door. I assumed that was for security reasons; of course, we were in no position to ask. Upon exiting the elevator, we were led outside to a waiting paddy wagon. As we stumbled in our attempt to get into the wagon, I said to my sister, "This is just like a horror movie, but only we are in it."

The paddy wagon looked like an ambulance on the outside but was very narrow inside. I raised my leg to get in the wagon, but because of the small space between my chained feet, I fell slightly over. No help from the guards. We were on our own. I managed to get both legs in after receiving a push from Candy. Finally, she could help me with something. We were in the back seated side by side. The court officers were in the front of the wagon with a gated partition as separation.

I knew how we were going to take that ride through the valley in shackles and chains. We were going to sing a song of inspiration. I belted out a song, "Victory is mine, victory is mine, victory today is mine. Joy is mine, joy is mine, joy today is mine. Peace is mine, peace is mine, peace today is mine."

I can only tell you that my singing on the way to the bubble was not a sign of arrogance; rather, it was a shield of protection. I needed my mind on something that made me happy. When I listen to inspirational music it reminds me that the joy of the Lord is my strength. I desperately needed my mind to be anywhere but in that paddy wagon facing that future.

The ride from the courthouse to the first jail-a round structure called the bubble- took about five minutes. When we arrived at the bubble, still shackled, the court officers opened the door to the paddy wagon and told us to step out. We almost fell trying to step down with the shackles on our feet and handcuffs on our hands. We were led into the building and placed together in a small ten-by-five-foot cell. The officer in charge closed the door behind us and locked it. The sound of the jail door closing echoed with shivering finality. There was a toilet in one corner and a metal flat board to sit or lie on.

I had dressed in sweats and sneakers because I knew I was going to jail. Candy, who we had not thought would get jail time, had on a pantsuit and shoes. There were no other prisoners present in the bubble. It was cold and felt damp. The quiet was deafening. An officer sat at a desk outside of our cell. He said nothing to us as we sat for hours without food or heat.

Although in normal circumstances I have a phobia about using a toilet outside of my home, during the wait in the bubble, nature called. The cell we were in was not private. There were no doors to the toilet. I do not even know if it was clean. Candy stood at the front of the jail bars and shielded me as much as she could. With her hands still cuffed in front of her, she helped me pull my sweat pants down because I too was still shackled like a wild animal even though we were both behind locked bars. This was the beginning of many times to come when I had to maneuver with the shackles that restricted my physical movement. Had my enabling actions really resulted in this? Yes, I did it to my sister, and I did it to myself.

After I regained my composure, I realized I still had the tiny Bible that the court officer said I could keep. Candy somehow maneuvered taking it out of my sweater pouch. It was very small and fit easily in the palm of my hand. There was enough room between the two wrist cuffs for me to hold the Bible. I opened it up and began to read Paul's letter to the Ephesians. I focused on Paul's instruction for wisdom and walking in love. I did not know what to expect when we arrived in general population with other women, but I knew I needed wisdom and I wanted to show love. Then I read Romans 8:36-39 – I needed to believe that even though I had placed myself in a terrible situation and had to suffer the consequences, there was nothing that would or could separate me from God's love. I then read Psalm 27, a prayer of confidence. I have always been confident. I was determined that this journey would not change that as long as I waited on the Lord every day to renew my strength. I read these passages out loud so that my sister could hear and receive the same power I felt reading the Word of God.

After several hours, two male officers arrived. They were the same officers who had been present during my sentence. One officer opened the cell door and said, "Let's go." My sister and I shuffled out of the bubble. We were again led to the paddy wagon on to our next destination. Our brief but arduous stay at the bubble had come to an end.

No Place to Call Home

During my time of incarceration, I was shipped around like produce on a delivery truck to four different institutions. After sentencing, and the brief stay at the Bubble Candy and I entered Mercer County Correctional Center, also known as The Workhouse. I stayed there six weeks while I waited for a bed at the State Prison for women. Candy was released and went home after two weeks. The conditions were horrid: steel beds with scratched, bent metal; bathrooms with mold in the shower; asbestos in the ceiling and lead in the old worn mustard paint on the walls. My first week there I lost ten pounds. The food consisted of white stale bread, coffee that tasted like mud, hot cereal which was cold, uncooked meat, and watery fruit drink. Each morning we were summoned to the day room to pick up our trays to eat breakfast and the same occurred for lunch and dinner. We shared a room that looked like a barrack with twenty-seven other women. The showers were cold, and the bathroom toilets were exposed; modesty was nonexistent. During my stay, I witnessed guards having sex with inmates, guards threatening inmates, and a lot of yelling and cursing between guards and inmates.

The next stop was Edna Mahan Correctional Facility, the only State prison for women, for four months and then to Bo Robinson, a privately run halfway house, for six weeks and finally to Millicent Fenwick House, a less restrictive halfway house, where I stayed until I was released. Each place had differences but the similarities were evident: disrespect by the guards, terrible food, poor living conditions and women who wallowed in low self-esteem. I suspected many of them had faced issues of enabling and codependency.

THE WORKHOUSE

Mercer County Correctional Center (MCCC), also known as the Workhouse, would be our heaven or hell for the next several weeks; it was up to us to choose. I was in transition and would have to wait for a space to open up at Edna Mahan Correctional Facility, the women's state prison. I thought it sad that there was a waiting list to get into prison. While this was not the first realization of the severity of trouble my sister and I were in, it resonated to the point that my head thumped with pain.

On the way to the Workhouse, we rode down tree-lined streets. I recalled times during my two-year tenure at Commerce when I drove down the same streets in my car on official state business. There was a different appreciation for what I witnessed. I thought to myself, time and actions really do bring about a change. What once was a joyful ride to and from work, today felt like a dreadful ride to my execution. We eventually arrived at the facility in the paddy wagon and drove through the gates past the high fence with barbed wire. The outside of the building was nondescript. Once again, we exited the paddy wagon and again were led to a metal door. The officers knocked, and a voice came over the loud speaker, "Three for admittance."

On our way to the Workhouse, we had picked up a male inmate who we did not see until we exited the wagon. The door opened, and there stood an African-American female correction officer. As we moved toward the entrance, she said, with a stern voice and bad attitude, "Sit on the bench." We sat on the cold metal bench. The three officers entered another locked metal door, leaving Candace, the other prisoner, and me in the locked hall on the bench. It was January and cold. I was glad for the warmth of my sweat suit. We waited for quite some time in the cold, dark hallway before we were summoned, one by one, to be processed. In processing, we were fingerprinted and our pictures were taken, placing us in the computer as official residents of the Workhouse. All my adult life, I seemed to rush with little patience. My lesson in waiting and patience was beginning, and so was my understanding and healing of the enabling spirit that had brought me to this dark place.

STRIP SEARCH

When Candy left me in the hallway, I thought this might be the last time I saw her, but God was already working it out. We were not separated as we expected. After she was processed, it was my turn. The same female officer ordered me to "stand up." I stood up. I had quickly learned the rules of engagement. When an officer spoke, I listened. This was something I was not use to because I was usually the one giving the orders. Finally, after eight hours, the shackles and chains were taken off. Although my arms and legs felt lighter, my heart weighed heavy in my chest.

The officer ordered me into a small room with a bench, toilet, and shower stall. The room had a widow and open door so anyone, even male officers, could see inside. "Take off your clothes, everything."

I began to take off my clothes one item at a time and hand them to the officer, who checked them for contraband and then threw them on the floor. She stood and watched me. I felt violated and was mortified by the entire process. I moved quickly because I really wanted this part to be over.

I stood butt naked as the officer sternly rattled off, "Open your mouth, stick out your tongue, stand with your legs apart, raise your hands up over your head, now lift your breast up, now turn around and spread your legs, bend over to your waist, spread your cheeks, squat and cough." I tried to remember what she was telling me to do as she told me to do it. I was very nervous. After all, I was an attorney, former judge, Christian, mother, and wife who lived a very middle class life. What was I doing here? I did not get everything right the first time because she was calling the orders out so fast. She told me to squat again, and I did. This was a strange experience for me, but "promises, promises" popped in my head: God promised He would be with me in the midst of everything, even my strip search.

While this book is not about a religious conversion as a result of my troubles, I have to share that it was my faith in God that carried me through. I had been a Christian prior to this experience and prior to the activity which led me to prison. I, like many, lost my way and did not put what I had learned into practice. I fell down, and I thank God every day for picking me back up.

After the strip search ended, the officer handed me a small bar of soap, a small dingy white washcloth, a small dingy white towel, a cup, which held a "security" toothbrush (security means smaller than the normal size toothbrush), a small tube of toothpaste and one small roll of deodorant. The officer said in her consistently cold, stern voice, "Take a shower." I walked over to the shower stall and turned on the water. As the water hit my body, I shivered. It was freezing. The days of hot showers were gone. As I showered without a shower curtain and the officer watched, I whispered to myself, "I can do this; I can do this." It is amazing how your mind can send you into survival mode when you are faced with life or death, and I wanted to live.

I dried myself and she handed me an orange jumpsuit along with white underwear, socks, and orange sneakers. "Put this on." Again, I submitted to the orders. Submission is not necessarily a sign of defeat; in certain situations, it is a sign of survival. This was not the time for me to protest the obvious demeaning and disrespectful acts taken against me. I had to think and act smart if I wanted to survive. This was not my side of the fence, but I was on it and I had to adjust. Unknowingly to me, this was yet another small step in the direction of my healing as an enabler.

After I dressed, I was directed to another holding cell and told to enter. Fear did not enter my mind but isolation did, moving through a maze of the unknown was difficult. I was alone and really wanted my family. Candace was in the next cell waiting for me. I was glad to see her, even for a moment, as I passed by her cell and was placed in the next one. I knew my little sister was tough, but I still worried about her, even though I was experiencing my own hell. Eight hours had passed since sentencing. It was nearly 5:30 p.m., and I had yet to eat a meal. The attitudes of the correction officers did not make me feel that it was okay to ask for food or drink. So, I waited. Finally, a prisoner came with food. He slid the tray through a hole in the door: hot dogs, cold beans, and stale white bread with nasty, watery purple juice. I did not eat. From that moment, I realized I was going to have many days of forced fasting.

PROTECTIVE CUSTODY

We waited for hours next to one another in our cells. There was a lot of movement outside. I could hear other people being processed and doors opening and closing, but I could not see anything. I began to think about this journey as an exciting book that I was reading, one I could not put down. I wanted to know what was next. Finally, an officer came to the door and said, "Devereaux, step out. You're wanted in IA." IA is Internal Affairs. I followed the officer upstairs to a back office, where a female officer in plain clothes sat behind a desk. I sat in front of her, waiting for her to speak. She asked me if I wanted to be placed in protective custody because of my position as a former prosecutor and judge. I politely said, "No, thank you." I understood protective custody to mean isolation where I would be placed in a cell by myself with a cot and toilet and unable to communicate with others. I did not want to be separated from my sister or placed in a cell with twenty-three-hour lockdown and restricted movement.

The counselor appeared to be a Christian woman. She had several posters on her wall with spiritual quotes and images. We began to talk about the path that life takes you. I expressed to her that while I understood I had to repay my debt to society through incarceration, I believed I was there at this appointed time on a specific God assignment, which was to bring hope into someone's life - to lead the women to accept Jesus Christ as their Lord and Savior. I told her I realized I might have to suffer for a while, but these were light afflictions. I knew how I handled my present circumstance would have a direct impact on someone else's life. She shared with me that her son had been arrested and imprisoned in the same facility that she worked in, and God had set it up so that she would not have to be at work when it happened.

After our talk, she produced my phone list, which allowed me to call my husband right away, a process that normally would take several weeks. I thought to myself, I am already in protective custody, under the protection of God. It really is okay. He had encamped at least one angel around me. I was taken back down to the holding cell and felt myself smiling inside. God's promises were starting to manifest. Shortly thereafter, it was time for Candy and me to be moved to the "tier," (also known as the cell block where the women prisoners reside) where we would reside for an uncertain time. When we arrived on the floor, my phone privileges were in place. We were able to call the family right away. That was my confirmation that we were not alone and this journey would not be a waste of time.

SISTER TO SISTER

Although there are several types of relationships that can produce enabling behavior – child to enabling parent, parent to enabling child, husband to enabling wife, wife to enabling husband, teacher to enabling student, friend to enabling friend, boyfriend to enabling girlfriend, girlfriend to enabling boyfriend, employee to employer– mine involved my family.

It is rare to have both the enabler and enabled end up in "physical" (emotionally they are both imprisoned by their conduct) prison at the same time. While this is an extreme circumstance, it is very real. I had totally lost myself in my sister's problems and did not realize it until it was too late. During this ordeal my sister and I became very close; she has given me permission to talk about her prior challenges, (She has also been delivered from the grips of enabling) in order to help others who may have issues with enabling. Candace is the youngest of the family. We call her Candy. As a child, she was sheltered by my mom and spoiled by everyone else. In her teenage and young adult life, she struggled with issues of low self-esteem and self-worth, never working to her fullest ability to accomplish her goals. We have discussed it and concluded that part of her problem was that she always lived in my shadow and was reminded of how she should do things better or like me. Mommy, in her pride over my accomplishments, at times forgot that Candy and I were different. As an adult Candy eventually developed a poor attitude, poor work habits, and a lack of responsibility over her finances. When issues became more than she wanted to deal with, she ran, eventually settling in another State.

During her time in North Carolina, she had a few bad relationships and lost several jobs. By this time, she had two children who needed care. While she tried to keep her problems secret from me, my mother constantly complained and worried about her daughter and her grandchildren. There were times when Candy and the children were padlocked out of their home and times when they slept on the floor of a friend's house.

Candy kept falling on hard times, and in many instances, it was a result of her own choices. Wrong choices in men or wrong decisions she made. Every time she fell, my mother and I were there to eventually pick her back up. She exhibited self-destructive behavior, and my mother and I came to the rescue – a classic enabling characteristic.

What I did not immediately realize was that with all of Candy's weakness, she too was an enabler as a result of the larger issue of codependency. Candy seemed to choose men who were worse off than she. In many ways, it boosted her self-esteem because she felt superior to the person who needed her. Candace's last dysfunctional relationship prior to prison was with an alcoholic. No matter how badly he exhibited toxic behavior, she chose to stay because she felt that she could fix him. (Two individuals with negative self-worth latching on to one another-codependency) We all knew he was bad for her, but she refused to see it. When she hit rock bottom in the relationship, my mother and I came to the rescue, (Two individuals hopelessly entangled with an out of control situation-enablers).

Candy knew no one would understand how she could be with a man and still struggle. All the while Candy was making a bad situation worse because she refused to hold the man in her life accountable for his actions and she lived in denial about hers. Unfortunately, neither Candy nor her mate was able to emotionally support one another or effectively enhance each other's life.

THE NEED FOR DISTANT LOVE

If you have siblings, is your relationship with your brothers and sisters a healthy one or do you find yourself constantly excusing their behavior and picking up the pieces of their lives? A person may need to fall in order to emerge stronger. If you are always there to pick a person up when he or she falls, you will eventually end up on the ground with that person. The sister-to-sister or sibling-to-sibling enabling relationship is hard to overcome, especially if you are the older sibling or the more mature sibling. You feel the need to protect and take care of your sibling. Instead of dominating the relationship, stand back and allow your siblings to do what they need to do for themselves. This might require distant love, meaning you cannot engage yourself in your siblings' everyday trials and tribulations. They have to realize that you will not always be there to help. They must learn to pick themselves up.

During my time as an enabler, I did not recognize the danger signs as they related to my own life. I never thought I had a problem. I was the problem-solver who was always quick to respond and take control of the situations that affected Candace's life. I totally missed the fact that the more I addressed her issues, the more I disregarded my own issues of control, anger, never thinking I was good enough, and trying to fit in. I had to learn distant love for my sister.

TWO LEFT

My first interaction with women as an incarcerated woman was approaching. Candy and I were on our way to the tier—an entire building of enabled people. County Jail was old, gloomy, and big. The walk down the long, dark jailhouse hall to the tier was scary because we had no idea where we were going. Candy and I each held in our arms a gray blanket, two white twin sheets, a washcloth, a towel, and toiletries in a cup. We traveled through a series of doors, following the male officer. Every door we entered was unlocked to let us in and locked behind us to keep us in. The clanging of the keys had a strange and cold echo. At first, the hall was quiet, but the closer we came to our destination the louder the noise became. We entered one last door, and suddenly the sound of loud talking, cursing, and yelling became very real. We had arrived at our final resting place, at least for the immediate unknown future. My heart raced. I felt squeamish like there was a large pit in my stomach.

I said to Candy, "And it begins."

She responded, "I know."

The tier was divided into four sections. On the first level, there were two sides with approximately twenty-five to thirty women on each side. I later learned that the first-floor, left-side tier housed women accused of murder with high bails. They needed a lot of money to get out of jail. I was so glad that we did not stop on this level. We traveled to the second level. As we reached the top of the floor, several women ran to the cell bars anxious to see who was coming. I felt a sigh of relief when we were both directed to the same cell block, Two Left. That meant we would be together, I her protector and she mine. More women approached the bars to peer at us. As the gate was unlocked for us to enter, I heard someone yell, "Fresh meat." They were talking about us. I felt like I was going to be the next big meal for a bunch of vultures. We had arrived.

THE GREAT MEDIATOR

Although I felt a bit of trepidation, I could not stay in fear long. It was either survive or succumb to the environment. Like many people, I had my impression of women in prison. I heard they were tough, bitter, and angry. Most were not remorseful for their behavior, and they liked to fight. I have always been pretty tough, not afraid to stand up for myself, but this was different. In my old world as an attorney, the tongue was the sharpest weapon. In my new world, the fist was the only weapon.

These women did not know my sister or me, but they knew we were not from their neighborhood or side of the tracks. That was evident by the way we looked and talked. Most of the women wore years of abuse, hardship and pain on their faces. Many of them were functionally illiterate. Candy and I both used proper grammar, and the look of weariness the others wore was not evident on our faces. My mission was survival and transformation. The most important assignment for Candy and me was to stay alive. We had to find a way to connect with these women without losing who we were.

I decided to embrace my fellow inmates with what I consider a common mediator: prayer. If they were receptive, that might break the ice. For those who were not, it might make them hesitate, thinking I had some connection with God. My hope for transformation was twofold. After all that I had been through, I did not intend for it to have been in vain. I refused to be bitter, angry, or shameful of my situation, and I wouldn't let anyone hold me hostage to my past. I had a wonderful opportunity to share and not be selfish. I had been accused of being selfish when word of my troubles hit the news, and upon reflection, I probably was a little selfish in not thinking of the impact my actions might have on others. My transformation, I hoped, would come from helping these women and not judging them. Transformation for the women was what I was most excited about. However, my approach toward helping the women would be different from the actions I took to help Candace. The dysfunctional enabling behavior that I engaged in was gone. The women's' bad behavior would not be rewarded. If they did not respond to the positive reinforcement I provided then I would just leave them to my prayers, which I should have done with Candace. I looked forward to meeting my sisters in prison and helping those who sought a change in their life. I was under no illusion that after years of struggle and adversity that any one of these women would change overnight, but if I could plant a seed of happiness and hope even in prison, my mission would be accomplished.

Our cell block held twenty-seven women with convictions for

various crimes: drugs, prostitution, theft, and assault. I wondered who had enabled them or who they had enabled. Obviously, there had been a course of continuing negative conduct that led them to this place. No matter how cool and collected I tried to be, it would not be difficult to figure out that I had never been in jail. Newbies stuck out, especially in jail. Here we were all equal; we'd all lost our freedom. I felt it was important to make my fellow inmates feel at ease. I said, "Hi, ladies." Most of the women spoke and immediately recognized the resemblance between my sister and me. A couple of them asked if we were twins. "No," I said, "I am the big sister, and she is the little sister." Prior to our incarceration, I had decided I would not talk about what brought me there. I figured my fellow inmates would hear about it on the news or from the guards. I did not need to talk about it.

With the stories that I heard and my own preconceived prejudices, to my surprise the women welcomed us and helped us get settled on our bunks. Candace was initially on a top bunk close to the bathroom, which was wide open. I was two bunks down on the top bunk with a bright light directly over my head. The tier was set up barracks style with seven old and worn bunks on each side of the room. There were rusty metal lockers in between the beds but not enough for each woman.

My "bunky," as we referred to the inmate, who shared the upper or lower bunk, was Lane. She slept below me. Lane was an older white woman. At least she appeared older because of the worn look and wrinkles in her face. She was anxious to help me. I appreciated it. Lane made my bed and tied a sheet behind the head of the bunk so I could store my few personal items. I have always believed in prayer, but during the years prior to the trial, I prayed often and alone. I wanted to pray with the women, but I was not sure how they would receive me.

I said, "My prayer is 'Lord, please provide me with the strength to begin this journey. "Is there anyone who would like to join Candace and me in prayer?" There were about ten women who ran to the circle. We held hands and bowed our heads. With eyes all closed, it was my prayer that God would touch each heart and strengthen them where they were weak. I prayed for their families, their court cases, and forgiveness. After prayer, the tone was set. Whatever the women's initial thoughts of my sister and me, they were quickly overcome by the power of prayer. It is a great mediator.

PEACE IN PRISON

Later that night, one of the ladies who had been lying on her bunk all day reached her hand out to me and asked me to pray for her because she was depressed. I prayed. She cried. I immediately realized that group prayer was fine, but each woman had specific needs. As the nights and days progressed, one by one, several women approached me and asked for prayer. My bunky, Lane, cried and asked me to be her pen pal after she was released because she wanted to stay grounded in the Lord. She was on her way home and did not know what to expect or how to handle her weakness to drugs. Trina, in for assault, was in the bunk directly across from me. She sought my spiritual counseling. Arlene, who sold drugs for many years and was fed up and mad at God because she believed He did not hear her, asked for prayer. As crazy as it sounds, my first day in exile seemed blessed because the women needed something that was obviously missing in their lives. While prayer is not always a quick fix, it was a beginning to meeting their needs. This was a healthy enabling because I was allowing myself to be the vessel that God used to help them.

That first night, I woke up around 3:00 a.m. I felt a nudge on the inside, which I can only attribute to God. It was finally quiet as I walked down the middle aisle of the bunk beds. All of the ladies were asleep – no cussing, screaming, or arguing. Peace in prison – an interesting concept. I realized that the only time there would be peace in this place was when everyone was asleep. As I touched each woman's bunk, I asked God to cover her and to remove whatever troubles there are in her life. I returned to my bunk, climbed back on my bed, and stared up at the ceiling. Finally, I closed my eyes, resting in my thoughts—peace in prison.

THE PAIN OF THE ENABLED

Nicole is in her early twenties. A thin, almost frail young woman, she has long black hair and looks years beyond her age. She has been on drugs, specifically heroin, for several years. She has no idea how to quit and is in forced detoxification by the mere fact that she is in jail. Her offense this time is possession of drugs. When she is not in jail, Nicole lives with a friend; she is allowed to stay, without paying rent or assisting with the other bills in the home. Nicole is waiting for the same enabler, I mean friend, to make bail for her, and she is depressed because it has not yet happened.

Nicole exhibits a classic sign of one who has been enabled. She has friends in her life who are aware of her addiction but continue to allow her to exist in it. This leaves little hope that Nicole will ever be free from her own weakness. She obviously has experienced a lot of pain in her life, and her only way of coping has been to rely on drugs. The question is: Does Nicole really have any friends if they allow her to continue with this type of destructive behavior? Her addiction has been fueled by her pain and perpetuated by those around her who continue to ingratiate her by ignoring her bad behavior.

IMAGE

Part of my experience has caused me to reflect to my teenage years where for the first time I noticed that my family was dysfunctional, but not to the point that it shifted my way of thinking. Recounting an important stage in your life, as I do here, is necessary toward understanding where the root of your enabling stems from.

Wow, at seventeen I am really graduating from high school. Through all of the dysfunction in my family, I am glad I stuck to my plan. I liked learning, but three years of high school is enough. I am so glad that through hard work and dedication, I am able to graduate early. I have so many dreams, so much I want to accomplish. There is a big wonderful world that I have read about and that I long to see, but first I have to go to college. Meme, my grandmother, won't have it any other way. Spelman College, a historically Black college for women, accepted me, so off I go. I will be the first grandchild to graduate from high school and complete college. Life at home has not always been easy. I have played mother to my older brother and younger sister for so long. Mommy is not to blame; she just did what she had to do. Virtually a single mother because of my father's drug addiction, she needed to work two jobs in order to provide for us. Even though we never really talked about her struggles, I saw what she went through. This truly is my motivation for wanting to succeed in life. I am an old soul. I feel adult enough to handle anything. My life is going to be great. I will major in communications and have a career in journalism just like Barbara Walters.

What a milestone. I think I can count the times my grandfather, Pop, has had a full conversation with me in my entire life. I think it has to do with the failures of his son, my father. Today is my graduation, and he is all smiles. I want him to be proud of me. I place a lot of pressure on myself to succeed because of the deficiencies of my father. Today, I have made everyone smile; everyone is happy that I graduated. I look forward to being able to provide for my family and for what life holds for me.

REFLECTION EXERCISES:
CHAPTER ONE

If you felt like you were in a bubble with your family, friends, or partner, what was the experience like for you?

_____

_____

_____

Metaphorically, if you have been stripped down to nothing at some point in your life, how did you cope with your feelings?

_____

_____

_____

If there is someone you feel obligated to help, yet feel drained by doing so, what can you do to alleviate some of your burden of care?

_____

_____

_____

If you have ever said to yourself, "this is the last time I will help this person," yet continued to help, how did your lack of follow-through make you feel?

_____

_____

_____

Do you see yourself as a "fixer" or as a "helper?" Describe the difference between the two.

_____

_____

_____

If you often seek out someone to step in to solve your problems do you often have one person in mind? What makes you choose this person?

_____

_____

_____

If your life has been absent of any real peace, how long have you allowed yourself to exist without it and is someone else responsible for the lack of peace in your life?

_____

_____

_____

You just finished "Imagine" in chapter 1. Take a moment and focus on your thoughts and emotions. If you are feeling uncomfortable emotions at this time, you might need to take a break before reading the next chapter. If you take a break, focus on achieving happiness and what it would take to reach it.

Chapter Two
CAGED BIRDS

*"When you give another person the power to define you,
then you also give them the power to control you."*
-Leslie Vernick

WOMEN IN JAIL defined as inmates are caged birds, desperate to fly
and sing to their own tune. We think it is the bars that contain us,
but it is so much more. If we leave this place the same enablers or
enabled as we came in, have we really escaped the cage?

CANDY THE CRANE BIRD

My sister Candace reminds me of the crane bird with its long legs,
neck, and bill. They spend most of their time wading in the water,
never really going out into the deep. They are opportunistic feeders,
changing their habits depending on the season. As a young adult,
Candace never really felt strong enough to launch out into situations
that would propel her to the next level of growth and responsibility.
I do not remember ever talking with her about what she wanted to
be when she grew up. She waded in the shallow waters of life with
no real interest in making any moves. An extremely moody person,

she changed with the day. She was constantly in my shadow, and in my opinion, this led to many of the negative choices that she made.

I woke around 7:00 a.m., right before breakfast. The realization slammed into me: Wow, Candace and I were really in jail. I looked over at my little sister on her bunk bed dressed in orange. She was still asleep. Although I realize now that I was not, I could not help but feel totally responsible for placing her in this position. Was this really part of my enabling tendencies? Candace has had her ups and downs in life and done a lot of things in secret to survive. But as God is my witness, this time she really was trying to do the right thing. I had approached Candace in an attempt to help her gain work independently and legitimately. She actually did a good job with the assigned projects. She had no idea that there was a problem until all hell broke loose. I was the one who offered her work. I was the one who used poor judgment in not following proper procedure. If I am honest with myself and my little sister, giving her the contract did nothing to help with her personal issues. Instead of taking control of her situation, I should have been encouraging her to do what she needed to do in order to provide for her children. This would have promoted self-sufficiency in Candace instead of dependency.

THE IMPORTANCE OF ALLOWING FOR SELF-SUFFICIENCY

A self-sufficient person makes room for suggestions in her life, but she does not convert that to dependency. Enablers don't allow self-destructive people to be self-sufficient. Instead, the enabler becomes intrusive in the lives of those who appear weaker than they are. For a long time this was the only interaction I knew to have with my sister. Through my conversations with the women in jail, I discovered that many of them had never lived self-sufficient lives.

There was always someone there to hold their hand or to tell them what to do.

GAILYN THE GULL

A gull bird is an acrobat capable of seemingly impossible antics that position its body at just the right angle while sometimes appearing motionless. Gailyn truly mimicked a gull bird. She knew just how to position her mouth to hide her daily medication. I cannot count the number of times during the call for medication that she would run to the front of the line for pills that she really did not need. Seroquel and OxyContin were both strong narcotics, which either put you to sleep or in a stupor, Gailyn flew to the line to receive her daily dose. It was the habit of the guards to dispense the meds, as they were called, and then with a stern voice command, "Swallow, open your mouth, stick out your tongue, now take your fingers and spread your cheeks." This order was given to make sure that the women did not hide the meds in their mouth instead of swallowing them. Gailyn was a master at hiding the meds by pretending to swallow.

Once she was back at her bedside, Gailyn would cough up her meds, dry them off, and sell them to the highest bidder. There was always an inmate willing to purchase the drugs by giving up her commissary. On occasion, Gailyn the Gull would ingest her own narcotics and lay on her bunk in a stupor, motionless for most of the day.

Gailyn is a prime example of a woman who has never led a self-sufficient life. She is a twin. Her sister was also in jail on the second floor at the same time we were there. No stranger to jail because of her drug addiction, she has been a frequent visitor of the Workhouse. During my stay at the Workhouse, I began to know the women and understand their pain. Gailyn shared with me that she grew up in Trenton, New Jersey in a rough area. She was raised by her grandmother, and when not in jail, Grandma always allowed Gailyn to return home.

Through all of her actions, Gailyn exhibited dependent behavior. Being dependent means Gailyn relied on people and unhealthy situations for support. She was dependent on drugs in order to face life. She was dependent on her grandmother in order to live life, and she was dependent on the prison system in order to survive. Self-sufficiency would have allowed Gailyn to maintain herself without outside aid. She would have been capable of providing for her own needs and been confident in her own ability and self-worth.

Gailyn was the enabled, and sadly her grandmother reinforced her bad behavior. She allowed her granddaughter to use her as a crutch. Gailyn had no incentive to establish independence. She knew Grandma would be her supplier when she was out in the street doing drugs, when she went to jail, and when she returned home. Grandma was the worst kind of supplier. She was the enabler.

BIRDS OF A FEATHER FLOCK TOGETHER

As the day began, I sat up in my bunk and looked at the women around me. They varied in age from the youngest (a girl of eighteen) to the oldest (maybe me at forty-nine my bunky, Jane, at whatever age). There were Hispanic, Black, and White women. Most were repeat offenders. Statistics point to the majority of women in prison as minority, so I was surprised to see so many white women of varied socio-economic backgrounds. I wondered, how did we get here? How did we allow ourselves to become so low that the only place that seemed fit for us during this time in our lives was a cell?

As an enabler, I had come full circle. Taking risks and not considering the consequences had turned into my biggest nightmare. I had always been a risk taker and felt that the only way that I could grow was to step out into the unknown and spread my wings. I did not, and still don't, necessarily think this is a bad thing. The challenge was not stepping so far out that you fell off a cliff. That is what I did. I did not give myself time to think about the risk I took; I just leaped. My behavior hurt many people. While there are many different women in jail, to some extent we were birds who flocked together because of our inability to say no.

Risk Takers

The women in jail have taken their own risk by experimenting with drugs and committing crimes. None of them considered the consequences of their actions, and now they were in a continuous cycle of suffering. I think all the women had multiple character traits of both the enabler and the enabled as well as major insecurities including low self-esteem. It is impossible to do drugs and feel good about yourself at the same time. You may have a temporary state of euphoria, which causes you to block out the real pain in your life, but when you recover, the hurt and pain are still very present. In talking with the women, they understood that what they had attached themselves to was wrong and unhealthy, but they persisted in their conduct because it helped them avoid facing the other issues within their life. They had given up on themselves and on life. As I began another day, from a different lens as one who once enabled, I thought about the loss of hope of the enabled women and wondered what I could do to make a difference.

In our circle time that morning, I shared with the women that if they wanted a changed life, they had to take hold of the tools that would help in their transformation. I tried every day to use inclusive language because I wanted them to know that I felt their pain and I could relate because I, too, am a caged bird. Lesly the Loon. Just like the bird, I feed by diving in. My hunger is satisfied when I am in someone else's life, working their problems out for them. Powerful and agile, like the loon, I am able to adapt to any situation. This had not always worked well.

As circle time progressed, the women and I acknowledged that we had committed errors in our life, which at some point landed us in jail. We talked about the weakness of the mind and flesh, and how it can lead to unhealthy behavior. I found myself facing hard realities about my own life and weaknesses. Weakness of the flesh does not have to always concern sexual desires, just selfish desires. In my own life, I had been selfish on a number of occasions, not stopping to think about how my desires might affect those whom I know and love. So my reality was that, in part, my selfishness had resulted in my hiatus in jail. If we are willing to take a hard look at our lives and become honest about our failures and shortcomings, then we make room for acceptance, healing, and change. Yes, there is the possibility that we can recover from the things that have made us leap off of the cliff without considering the consequences. Enablers and enabled—we both have to look before we leap.

BIRD CAGE KEEPER

Now that my wings had been clipped, the guards become significant in my life. They were charged with watching the inmates and keeping order in the confined space. It got crazy in there on a daily basis. I woke up to noise, and I went to sleep to noise. Cursing was the preferred way to communicate and fights were always a possibility with tempers flaring because of the close space. I truly felt like I was in a cage and that was what the guards called the area where we were housed.

I had been there a few days, and I was puzzled regarding what the guards really did. Each one came into the tier, cursing, calling us names, and threatening us with lockdown—most of the time for no reason. This constant verbal abuse of women, who were already out of sorts, seemed to me like the guards were throwing salt on a wound. The guards were the bird cage keepers. They fed us and locked us in at night. The other women didn't seem to mind the barrage of daily insults. It was almost as if they felt some kind of needed acceptance from the guards. I came to realize that the guards were enablers as well. Behavior that borders on disrespect of those you are enabling and the person being enabled accepting this behavior were classic signs of an enabling relationship. The women were receptive to the abuse and readily received it. The guards dished out disrespect and, without realizing it, became the enablers to the women in prison.

One day a male guard was on duty. He seemed to enjoy disrespecting the women. He appeared to have some familiarity because most of the women were repeat offenders. From the outside of the locked cage, the officer yelled, cursed, and called the women names. I called a prayer circle—that is when all of the ladies gather in the tier in a circle holding hands and I prayed for them. The circle was getting bigger by the day, and that day there were about twenty women. I led prayer, as usual, speaking as loud as I could, trying to block out the cussing and screaming that echoed in my ears. For the women in the prayer, this was the only time they got to focus on something other than the negative atmosphere that was constant morning, noon, and night. At the end of the prayer, the women clapped, not for me, but as affirmation for the prayers. The correction officer standing outside of the cage said in a loud, cynical voice, "Your prayers don't matter. You still will end up back in jail." What happened next shocked me: Some of the ladies responded with laughter; others joked and cursed at him. I stood there thinking: How can they think anything he said was funny? Their response to his disrespectful, degrading comments suggested to me that the women were comfortable with being humiliated because this had been their reality for a long time. Whether in prison or on the streets, these women have been constantly ridiculed and demeaned by the very people who profess to love and protect them. The exchange between the guard and the women could only be termed abusive. The negative interaction and exchange lasted until that excuse for a man left.

I shared my observations with the women during our nightly Bible study. I told them that it was important that they try to start thinking more highly of themselves, that prison was not a reason to accept negative remarks. That night my prayer for the women was that they realize what binds them mentally, physically, and spiritually. Once they realize what binds them, they may begin to understand that they can be free from their limitations no matter how enabled they have become. The power to change is internal and not in anything they can do on their own; they must reach for something higher and stronger. As I looked at the women, I thought, some of them really want change in their life, but they just do not know how to begin the process for change, which will unfortunately continue to place them in a state of dependency.

CAGED BIRDS AND THE CYCLE OF DEPENDENCE

Angelyn Miller, author of the book The Enabler, said, "When people with irresolvable problems turn them over to others to handle, and there are willing takers, the cycle of enabling dependence begins." The women in prison were all victims of a cycle of dependence. They existed mentally and emotionally in a state of influence and control by something or someone else. In many cases, the dependence was a result of an emotional trauma, which had caused the person to believe that whatever the problem, it was too much for them to manage. What is interesting about this thinking is that the trauma, whether self-induced or forced, is what the enabled person is unwilling to address.

Dependency is not always a bad thing as long as it stays healthy.

We are born into the world dependent on our caretakers for survival. As we mature in the natural order of things, those whom we have been dependent on are supposed to gradually loosen the grip and allow us to learn to fly. It is our natural instinct to want and need a sense of dependence from others. Family bonds are nurtured with the security of knowing that if they have no one else they have each other. Children develop the need for depending on their parents. The roles seem to reverse when parents age and the dependency shifts. Employers are able to run their businesses effectively if they can depend on their employees for performance. Married couples depend on each other for emotional support when forming a family unit and building their lives. When people are ill, they depend on others to assist them in what they are unable to do. In looking at the cycle of dependency, it really extends beyond the family and friend unit into the world. In some way, big or small, we are all dependent on one another in order to co-exist.

Healthy dependency is justified in many situations of life. But even the person who has been stricken ill and now recovered is eventually expected to resume his or her independence when physically able. Children are expected to leave home when they reach the age of maturity. Elderly parents usually fight to maintain their independence, and if at all possible, they usually win the battle. Even married couples joined together for better or worse desire a certain amount of independence in order to preserve their own identity.

But what happens to the caged bird, the person who uses her tragedy or setback in life to keep her on a vicious cycle of dependency surrounded by emotional bars? She has convinced herself that her issue is insurmountable. Ultimately, the caged bird justifies her behavior and settles in to her nest allowing others to control her life.

From the eyes of an enabler (that used to be me), I now see how my actions in dealing with an unhealthy dependent is detrimental for the dependent and tragic for me. This may sound crazy, but as I sat in jail surrounded by unhealthy dependents with self-destructive behavior, there were days when I wished I could take them all home and care for them, "fix them." That was me – Lesly the Loon Bird – a classic enabler.

LIZZY THE LARK

Lizzy truly has the melodious voice of a lark. Early in the morning she rises, and you can hear her beautiful voice belting out a religious melody above the cursing and yelling. But like the lark, Lizzy is fragile and in need of care.

Lizzy is twenty-seven years old, pretty, overweight, and loud. She told me that she grew up going to church with her grandmother. The church was strict and she could not wear pants or makeup. As peer pressure set in, she rebelled and stopped going to church. I said, "Lizzy, I want you to sing like that for the Lord." She smiled and said okay. I sat next to her, and she began to tell me about her life and how hard it was for her growing up. Abandoned as a young child by her crack addict mother, Lizzy lived with her grandmother until the age of ten. When she finally reunited with her mother, it was a terrible experience. Lizzy shared how her mother would disappear for days, leaving Lizzy with the mom's boyfriend, who sexually abused her. Telling her mother meant nothing and only started arguments and filled the house with anger. Eventually, Lizzy's mother got rid of the man, and Lizzy and Mom started doing drugs together. Lizzy started dealing drugs and giving them to her mother. When Lizzy got busted and landed in jail, her mother would bail her out so that they could resume their activity – Lizzy supplying drugs to her mother and her mother supplying a place for Lizzy to live. The abuse really messed Lizzy up, but I think her mother was the bigger culprit.

I thought about my own molestation drama at the age of twelve – two different men on different occasions. I felt ashamed for many years and often blamed myself. I did not think I could talk to anyone about what occurred so I suppressed the events until adulthood.

The problem with secrets is that they have a way of eating at your soul. It is a tragic event, something that can easily leave you dependent and affect your personal relationships. As a result of my tragic experience, I became a control freak, determined not to let anyone have any kind of power over me again. I had no voice when these encounters occurred, but, I thought, from now on I would be in control of my life and without even realizing it exerting control over others. I became a habitual enabler.

Absent of the drug addicted mother, (My mom never used drugs), Lizzy and I had similar experiences but our emotional approach was different. I became an enabler; she, the enabled. I managed to move past my experience in a productive way by excelling in education and professional endeavors. But that need to intrude in the problems of others was there even if not self-evident. Lizzy used drugs and sold her body for money trying to escape from the pain, eventually embarking on a vicious cycle. The irony is that we both ended up in jail.

As the one who enabled, I did not realize that my own insecurities and the tragic events that took place in my life resulted in me deflecting what I felt on others. I thought I was in a healthy way because I did not comprehend that I had my own lack of self-worth. You will notice that my definition of dependence included the reality that we all need each other. I never felt I needed anyone.

Lizzy is the classic unhealthy dependent. During our talk, she always made excuses for her present situation: blaming the men for molesting her, her mother for being an addict, her grandmother for being too strict. While she has a legitimate claim relative to the abuse and even her mother's conduct, how she chose to process the problems is what continues to land her in jail.

As an unhealthy dependent, Lizzy spends most of her energy on the problems in her life—and not a solution. Her fear of finding answers for herself limits her ability to move past self-demise. As long as she has someone to depend on when she goes home (grand-mother or even her mother), she has no incentive to change. Mom needs Lizzy for drugs, and Lizzy needs Mom because she perpet-uates her behavior. Grandma is just there to pick up the pieces, and even without condoning the activity, she will not or cannot do anything to change it. Grandma's hope is in the false reality that somehow she can make Lizzy better. Lizzy is a caged bird, comfort-able in her very existence. Her only way out is to fly.

My introduction to the ladies, who I describe as birds, was short but meaningful. As I prepared to transfer to a different facility I took each of their stories with me and prayed constantly for their total healing. I left MCCC with a very different view of incarcer-ated women.

REFLECTION EXERCISES:
CHAPTER TWO

What are your thoughts after reading about Gailyn the Gull? Do you see yourself in Gailyn or in her grandmother, the giver?

_____

_____

_____

Are you the enabled? Have you always been a self-sufficient person or have you relied on others to pick you up when you fell down?

_____

_____

_____

Are you like Grandma, ready and willing to come to the rescue of your family knowing what they are doing is wrong? Is your door always open?

_____

_____

_____

Is it more important for you to take the leap or to land on your two feet? Taking the leap means you react without thinking of the consequences. Looking before you leap allows you to prepare your-self for what lies ahead.

_____

_____

_____

If you have any problems like Lizzy the Lark, describe them.

_____

_____

_____

If you have any problems like Lesly the Loon, describe them.

_____

_____

_____

If you are like the Bird Cage Keeper Guard, explain.

_____

_____

_____

Chapter Three
THE FAMILY TREE

"My family is my strength and my weakness."
-Aishwarya Rai Bachan

THERE IS A phrase which says, you can choose your friends but you can't choose your relatives. I don't know where the phrase came from but I have often heard it as it relates to family members who at times cause conflict. In all honesty if I had my choice between a strong, hard-working family man as a father and one who struggled with addiction, my choice would have been the former. Daddy has been dead twenty six years now and I took care of him until the day he closed his eyes as a result of complications from lung cancer. As a child I was sad because of the lifestyle he chose. I did not realize at the time that his dysfunction affected the entire family: my brother's behavior because he starved for the attention of a father; my sister's low self-esteem because she embraced some of my father's characteristics; my mother's guilt and overcompensation toward my brother; my grandmother's pain because her son was not loved by his father; and my attitude because I had to shoulder all the responsibility of an adult while my mom worked and attended college. As an adult who has finally come to terms with my childhood reality,

I understand that my father's weaknesses played an integral part in the foundation of my strengths. Alternatively, his weaknesses which were coddled by my grandmother partially formed the basis of the enabling characteristics that I possessed: the need to control, the insecurity and low self-esteem.

As I have already shared, the 2004 indictment not only affected me but directly affected my mom, sister, husband, children and friends. The guilt set in quickly. I felt such remorse for causing an avalanche of pain for so many people. I experienced a period of deep depression, and even thought my life was not worth living. I went to my doctor who subsequently prescribed antidepressant medication. The medicine made me more depressed ready to act upon my suicidal thoughts, but a voice in my ear kept saying, "You can't leave your children." I am glad I heeded the voice because suicide is never the right answer.

However, other judgments invaded my mind. I was not able to escape thoughts of why I felt the need to help my family in the way I did. Why did I feel such pressure to rescue them? Why didn't I find another way to help them? The questions I asked myself extended to my actions toward friends and clients. As an attorney I was in the business of resolving problems. I felt comfortable in the role of the aggressive assertive advocate. As a friend I loved being the "go to girl." Now, this is not to suggest that any attorney is an enabler because of her aggressive or assertive behavior. Nor am I suggesting that if people come to you with problems that you have codependent issues. I am merely stating the mindset I carried and how the thinking affected my decision-making as it related to family and friends. There are some people who may relate.

The thoughts continued for quite some time. My behavior and the realization of my character weaknesses were not immediate but after several sessions of therapy, intense critical reflection, journaling and a look at my family dynamics I began to understand that the pressure did not come directly from my mother, sister or friends. The pressure came from me. As the one whom everyone looked to for resolution,

I thought it was my duty to respond. I don't mean to suggest that all people who are products of dysfunction commit crimes or become enablers. That is not true. It was, however, true for me.

Digging deeper, I asked myself the question, could the struggles of my family, which I had witnessed, have attributed to my poor decisions? Was there a learning system in the habits of my family which was passed down, one generation teaching those behaviors to the next generation? After outlining and reviewing my family tree, I have concluded that, yes, what I saw in my family members impacted me greatly as an adult. The women in my family have had the biggest influence on me, and it is because of the strength that I witnessed in them that I have been able to withstand the dark times in my life and experience the greatest joy.

MEME AND ME

My late paternal grandmother, Meme, was the glue that kept the family together. She had a significant impact on my life. My family always reminds me that I am just like Meme. My mother is my biggest role model. As I shared earlier she is a woman who has endured a lot of hardship in her life, but she kept going in order to improve her life and the life of her children and others. I believe I possess the strength they both exhibited. But there were other areas of their lives which I witnessed and mimicked, which carried into my adult life as an enabler.

When Meme met my grandfather, he was fifteen years her senior. She was fifteen, pregnant, and married, in that order. My grandparents had an emotionally distant marriage, and as a result, Meme suffered from attachment issues and lack of connectedness (two of the characteristics of a codependent). This emotional deficit resulted in my grandmother overcompensating in the lives of her children, grandchildren, and anyone else whom she believed needed her. My father was my grandmother's most challenging project. Even in my father's adult years, Meme felt the need to provide for him and picked him up every time he fell.

MY DAD DISAPPOINTED

My father was the last child between my grandparents. My grandfather and his mother did not hide the fact that my dad was not wanted. He was called ugly by his grandmother and his father never talked to him. (No wonder he suffered from low self-esteem.) Meme immediately began to shelter my dad in an attempt to make him feel loved, but the love that he needed was from my grandfather. Meme was hurt that Pop rejected my dad so she overcompensated when it came to the needs of my dad. Dad enlisted in the Army and returned home with an addiction to drugs. He had found something to ease his pain of rejection and low self-esteem. When my mother and father met, she did not know that he was addicted to drugs. He kept it a secret. When she realized that his long stays in the bathroom were because he was shooting drugs, she was devastated, and after many years of hiding the fact out of embarrassment and shame, eventually, mom put him out. After my parents separated, my father went to live with my grandmother, who had thus far done a good job of enabling him.

MIMIC

As children, we look to our parents and grandparents as role models. We want to be like them. We watch how they respond to various tasks and issues and usually carry that information with us. We use it to help us make decisions in our own lives. It was a sad thing to watch my father exist as a drug addict, and I was certain that I did not want any part of that in my life. So, instead, I watched and learned from my grandmother, whose actions were mostly good and always from a place of love. She always encouraged me to be better and to reach high in my accomplishments. As I matured, I watched Meme take care of my father as if he were still her little boy. She cooked for him, washed his clothes, cleaned his room, and opened the door if he forgot his key. Although she never mentioned the fact, Meme knew that my father was a drug addict, but I think she blocked it out because she thought if she helped him, by showing him love, he would change.

Learning to Enable

I continued to learn from Meme what it meant to care for people; everyone could depend on her. She could make you cry when she was angry and laugh when she was happy. Over the years, I watched as Meme opened her doors to many people who were down on their luck: alcoholics, people who had legal issues, people she allowed to move in and rent a room in the family house. There were several people who could not pay the rent, and she let them stay anyway, hiding this fact from Pop. On many occasions, she would use her own money to supplement the tenants' rent. She loved the company, the attention, and being loved by everyone. It filled a void and made her feel like she really mattered, (she did really matter because the entire family loved her beyond measure). It was evident by her actions and her words that she was not complete unless she was giving to others, even to her detriment. The very depths of her soul reeked sadness. She lived with the spirit of an enabler.

I watched and learned as Meme continued to care for people who were undeserving and inconsiderate. She constantly made excuses for bad behavior. One of my cousins was a drug addict and thief with violent tendencies. Meme slept with her pocketbook under her pillow because he had stolen from her in the past, yet on the occasions that he asked for money, she gave it to him never turning her back on my cousin. He always had a place to stay. In my adult years, I began to mimic Meme. She was the matriarch and I was like her, so I needed to operate like she did— learned behavior.

I don't believe that children are born bigots, or drug addicts, or killers, I think that there is something that they see or have experienced in their life that shifts their thinking and causes them to react to situations differently. This is not to say that all people who have negative experiences turn into bad people - quite the contrary. I think our experiences help shape us, but we make the final choice in which way we will go. However, some things are learned. Kids do not know prejudice unless they hear it in their home, on television, or with people they associate with. I don't think it is a stretch to see that becoming an enabler has something to do with what you saw in your family.

THE LOVE OF A SON

Mommy's struggles continued with my brother, Shawn, who was a year older than me. Shawn (whom my son is named after) really had no male role model; our father certainly wasn't one. At an early age, my brother cried out for attention. He started acting out, stealing his first car at age fourteen. Mommy did everything she could - getting him counseling, enrolling him in a military academy, even sending him to live with Meme, with no concept of what enabling involved. When my brother was in the youth detention center, Mommy would pack us up to visit him. When Shawn returned home, he would come back to our house or Meme's house. Money was repeatedly spent on lawyers and bail for Shawn mainly by Meme but sometimes by Mommy.

CANDY BABY

Candace is the baby, and you already know that she and I were in jail together for a short time. I believe that the relationship between my mother and sister has been the biggest example of enabling between family members. Candy was always quiet and observed things. She never had to accept any real responsibility in the home and never was disciplined by my mother or father. In her young adult years, she grew more dependent, even while living on her own. Candy made poor choices in men and usually ended up with someone who would not work. So she took care of her man and her children.

When her money was short, which was often, Candy would call Mommy or Meme and eventually, me. We all came to her rescue at different times. Eventually when her relationships failed, Candy moved in with Meme, into the very room on the third floor which my now deceased dad had existed. I say existed because he wasn't really living or thriving. Drugs had taken over his life and he merely existed for many years. Candy lived rent-free with Meme and handled her finances poorly. Candy eventually moved to North Carolina to escape the pressures she had placed on herself. She thought by moving away that everything would change, but she forgot that she took herself with her. In her later adult years Candy tried to keep her issues secret, but that was impossible because every time she needed money she called my mother, who in turn bailed Candy out. That's what enablers do - they constantly come to the rescue of others, never addressing their real problems, just patching up what is broken. Eventually, the patch wears out, and the enabler has to return to mend what has come apart.

FAMILY DYNAMICS

It is safe to say that the existence of codependent behavior involves an excessive preoccupation with the lives of others. Family dysfunction is the best teacher of this behavior.

As painful as it has been to share my family struggles I want you to see how a combination of family dynamics can propel you to act before you think, sending you on a downward spiral without you even realizing that is what is happening. My grandmother suffered from low self-esteem and attachment issues because of her relationship with my grandfather. Consequently, she enabled my father and whoever else she could manage to get her hands on. My mother, who never experimented with drugs, suffered from embarrassment, guilt, and shame because she had challenges in her childhood and married a drug addict. As a result she enabled my sister and brother. I suffered from anger about my life, feeling inadequate, and needing to control all situations pertaining to family, so I enabled everyone. Helping not only hurt the ones I love, but it hurt me, too. I stopped caring about myself and only cared about fixing others.

The women I spent ten months in prison with were victims of the family tree, too. I heard countless stories about abuse and drug addicted mothers, fathers, sisters, and brothers. I also witnessed Grandma, Auntie, a sister, a cousin – who would visit the women in jail, raise their kids while they were in jail, and allow them to return home to continue on the same course of negative conduct most of the time which involved repeat incarceration.

Enablers are repeat offenders just as much as the enabled is a repeat offender, a term used in the criminal justice system which means a person who habitually commits offenses, causing them to return to jail. The enabler habitually rescues the drug addict, alcoholic, and emotionally-troubled, makes excuses for them, and picks the enabled up when they fall.

REFLECTION EXERCISES:
CHAPTER THREE

You can look at your family dynamics by drawing your family tree. Start at the top of the tree with the oldest person that is deceased on your mother's and father's side – great grandparents, grandparents, parents, etc., List the names on each branch. Think about each family member's story and try only to focus on their strengths and weaknesses.

IS THERE A HISTORY IN YOUR FAMILY OF?

☐   DRUG ADDICTION ABUSE

☐   MENTAL ILLNESS

☐   PERSONALITY DISORDER

☐   ANXIETY

☐   THIEVERY OR MISCHIEF

☐   HABITUAL LIAR

Who is the person everyone turns to for help – mother, father, grandmother, grandfather, sister, brother? Who is the person who always comes to the rescue of those who behave badly - mother, father, sister, brother, aunt, uncle?

_____

_____

_____

List yourself on the family tree and decide what your role has been in the family dynamics.

_____

_____

_____

Try to find a connection between the strengths of family members and the weaknesses of family members.

_____

_____

_____

What did you learn from the behavior you saw in your family?

_____

_____

_____

Do you mimic the unhealthy behavior as much as you do the healthy behavior?

_____

_____

_____

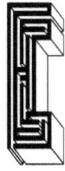

Chapter Four
WOMEN AND ENABLING

*"No matter what else they are doing
women are also always nurturing."*
-Cokie Roberts

WHY DO WOMEN care so much?
There is limited empirical literature on the issue of codependency. Most is clinical and theoretical. I come from a place of personal experience and behavior which I exhibited to draw my conclusion. Arguably, women make up a large majority of codependents in the world. The question is why do they care so much? The short answer is that the relationship is more important to them than they are to themselves. A more in-depth rationale seems to be related to nature and socialization.

In an article titled, Family Stressors as Predictors of Codependency, it is said that, "Women are traditionally known as nurturers and caretakers, because of the propensity to define themselves through their relationships and to view themselves through an external focus." Women care because of their instinctive nature to provide a nurturing environment for other human beings. Women care because they want to care; women care because it is the right thing to do; women care because no one else cares; women care because they need to care; women care because they were born to care.

The natural instinct to nurture is deeply rooted in a woman's very existence. In normal circumstances, as a small child, the first object of attachment given to a female is often a doll. At night, with her arms wrapped tightly around it, the child finds the doll is something to hold on to. It serves two purposes: first, it is something she can attach herself to, and secondly, her doll makes her feel safe and allows her to sleep without fear. Her doll is also someone she can love, nurture and protect. She controls the relationship which leaves her with a good feeling inside. It does not matter whether she is rich or poor. There always seems to be a doll of some sort in a young girl's life.

My mom did not have much money when we were growing up, but she found a way to make sure that my sister and I had a doll. I remember my first doll. She was larger than life sitting under the Christmas tree. I fell in love with her immediately because she was someone I could take care of. I combed her hair, washed her clothes, and made vain attempts to feed her. Instinctively, I felt this was what I was supposed to do. I could not let anything happen to her. I saw myself as her protector and could not let her fall into harm, nor could I allow anyone else to do what I believed I was supposed to do.

I imagine other little girls, maybe even you, have had similar feelings of nurturing with dolls and people, which placed you in a position of caring. There is nothing wrong with caring or nurturing. Every human being deserves some kind of nurturing. We all have a desire to be needed and to feel needed. Being needed means there is someone in the universe that relies on us. What we do for that person matters. This feeling of being needed is wonderful for our feelings of self-worth. It even lends itself to a certain amount of maturity and responsibility because we are accountable for someone other than ourselves.

Unfortunately, for some women the instinct of caring and nurturing has the potential to lead them into unhealthy relationships. A woman can find herself nurturing the wrong characteristics in people which produces weakness and negative energy that attacks the very depths of her thoughts, feelings, soul, mind, and spirit.

If you are nurturing a weakness in someone else, you have not dealt with your own weakness. Your weakness could be a result of years of engaging in volatile relationships, which resulted in a feeling of low self-esteem or self-worth. You have stayed in these unhealthy relationships because you have a basic need for affection, but in fulfilling this need, in this manner, you are denying your own self-worth. The baby doll in your life allows you to give and receive affection without damage to yourself; but if the baby doll is all that you have been able to garner affection from as a child, then in your adult years you most likely will have serious voids in your life.

Low self-esteem, loss of identity, a need for connectedness, and lack of personal boundaries are just a few of the personal challenges a woman may face, which is translated into her desire to overcompensate in another person's life to her detriment and others.

LOW SELF-ESTEEM

Suffering from low self-esteem can cause you to place more value in the life of someone else than in your own life. Low self-esteem has everything to do with how you view yourself, and nothing to do with how you view the other person. If a woman does not like what she sees in the mirror, she is likely to look to someone else to validate her. Taking control of another person's life and trying to fix that person, in some sense, empowers her. There is someone that she can view lower than herself. Thus, she has never really had the opportunity to focus on her own inadequacies because she is too busy focusing on the person whom she is enabling. She has become fixated on the enabled and begun making excuses for the bad behavior exhibited rather than holding the person accountable for what she knows is wrong.

While the feeling of worthlessness is part of the definition of low self-esteem, the result of low self-esteem can lead to potentially destructive behavior. The inability to say no presents a major problem for the enabler.

I sat in a prison full of women who suffered from low self-esteem and the inability to say no. Some of the women were enablers and some were enabled. The women who were enablers usually had a drug dealer boyfriend or pimp whom they supported and made excuses for him on a daily basis, thus perpetuating bad behavior. The women who were enabled were usually products of a controlling mother, father, or family member who made excuses for their continuous bad behavior.

I often wondered why these women would spend so much time in one-sided relationships to the point of giving up their freedom. But I had done the same thing without being in a one-sided relationship. I soon realized it is because generally speaking, in some instances women have been socialized and trained to behave in self-destructive ways that benefit men at the women's expense. My proof lies in the lives of the women I met in prison.

Misguided Gailyn

I mentioned Gailyn the Gull earlier. I spent a lot of time with her and believe that she is important as an example of a woman whose socialization started early, almost at birth. Gailyn suffers from low self-esteem and has been enabled most of her life. One night after Bible study, she sat on the floor next to my bed with her legs crossed. Trying to stay awake, I knew she wanted to talk; Gailyn opened up about her life and her twenty years of drug addiction. She was raised by her grandmother. Abandoned by her mother, she did not know who her father was. Gailyn began experimenting with drugs in high school. Marijuana use led to pills, which eventually led to crack cocaine. Gailyn surrounded herself with other drug addicts. As her habit increased, so did her desire to do whatever she needed to do to get drugs. She eventually dropped out of high school and started committing crimes to support her habit. Gailyn stole whatever she could sell, she robbed people for money, and she lied to get the drugs she needed to support her habit.

Gailyn is a small-framed woman and from her looks it is evident that the drugs have taken a toll on her body. She sold her body on several occasions to support her drug habit. This was not Gailyn's first time in county jail; in fact, it was probably her twentieth time for prostitution and possession of illegal narcotics. Gailyn spoke about her struggle with drugs and the many trips to rehab in an attempt to get clean. She told me that her challenge was not getting clean – it was staying clean. As tears rolled down her face, Gailyn's pain and anguish was telling. She felt trapped. As she sat on the concrete floor next to me in the cage, Gailyn made a shocking revelation: she told me that she really was not ready to leave the pit of hell that we were in. I was shocked because all I wanted to do was leave. She said that she was not emotionally prepared for what the outside had in store for her. Her self-esteem was so low that she believed herself unworthy to make it on the outside.

Gailyn's self-destructive ways were validated by family members over and over again during the prior twenty years of her life. When she became pregnant with her son and returned to the streets for drugs, her grandmother was there to raise her son. When Gailyn went to prison for committing crimes and was set to return home, there was always a family member ready to take her back. While it's clear that Gailyn was enabled, the surprising thing about her behavior is she also was an enabler. Gailyn was the older of her twin sister. As Gailyn shared her family story, I realized that initially Glenda did not exhibit the same behavior as Gailyn, but eventually she, too, turned to drugs. Gailyn fed her sister's addiction along with her own. She stole for her, lied for her, cheated for her, and even bought drugs for her, eventually landing them both in jail. They were identical twins with seemingly identical self-destructive behavior.

This was not unusual. There were other women with siblings

and even adult children on the tier with them. Sisters from the same bloodline locked away-Gailyn and Glenda, my sister and me - we were really not so different. We all had been socialized to believe that women ought to be a certain way. We watched, listened and learned that we were supposed to be in relationships and that we had to please everyone. Putting the needs of others before ourselves was expected behavior.

CONNECTEDNESS

Another debilitating trait of an enabler, and I would dare say the enabled person, is the need for connectedness. Somewhere in your life there was a time when you did not feel connected. The lack of connectedness may have been a result of a loss that you experienced in your life which left you starved for affection.

My father struggled with his own personal demons – low self-esteem and addiction problems – which left no time for him to care about how his children or wife felt. My grandfather, the true patriarch of the family, never engaged in conversation with my siblings or me and never once said he loved us. Imagine what this kind of deficit does in a person's life. To never hear words of love and affection from a loved one - parent or grandparent - makes a huge impact and it can leave you feeling empty. I believe that there is an innate need for all of us to hear the words that convey love. Simply providing for a family financially is not enough to meet the need. I've overcompensated for this void in my life by making sure I connected with others in my family who were struggling by placing myself in the middle of everyone's situation, whether they invited me in or not.

As a young girl, I learned how to control situations to garner attention. I made sure I did the best in all areas of my life and everyone knew I was the best. As an adult, I learned how to control situations by helping others. If my brother needed a place to stay, it had to be with me, regardless of the fact that he was unemployed. If my sister needed a job, I made sure I found her one, even though her poor attitude was the reason she could not keep a job. Neither of them had to take care of their own lives; I did it for them. I needed to feel connected, it drove me. There was too much sadness because of my father's addiction and my mother trying to keep it a secret. I knew my family depended on me and this made me feel loved and appreciated. Feeling love and appreciated was not the problem, but I contend that in some way the need to feel this way led to obvious poor choices in my life.

BOUNDARIES

The lack of boundaries is another area that I struggled with and which I believe is a characteristic of an enabler. Boundaries are defined as limits, the point at which something ends. Having adult responsibilities placed on me as a child set the stage for boundaries to be blurred in my life. For all intents and purposes, I was the adult and caregiver for my brother and sister while my mom worked. I was not a problem child so very rarely did my mother place limitations on me. I was use to inserting myself into the lives of my siblings. I believed it was expected and certainly accepted by my brother and sister. As an adult, my intrusive behavior became increasingly evident to everyone but me. Today I can admit that I was bossy and I still struggle with bossiness. As my brother and sister both experienced their own personal challenges which called for help from the family, I found myself in a position of not knowing when to say no to their request for help when things were going wrong in their lives.

Healthy personal boundaries are based on your own moral compass. Going against your values for another person means that you may want to reassess your relationship with that person. I did not ascribe to this principle. Instead of enjoying a healthy relationship with my brother and my sister, I perpetuated an unhealthy environment for myself and for them by not knowing when to say no. When my brother acted out and got in trouble with the law, I was always there to make excuses for him. When my sister messed up in school or lost a job, I helped her get through. There was no protection for me and none for them because when it came to finances, shelter, or protection, boundaries were invisible in our relationship.

For an enabler - characteristically one who has no boundaries - it is impossible for you to have a healthy relationship with anyone without trying to take control, especially someone who also does not have boundaries. The women that I shared my life with in prison were connected in an unhealthy way to people with no boundaries of their own. This situation was exacerbated by the imprisoned women not having a clear set of boundaries. The result was a toxic codependent relationship.

When dealing with issues of enabling, women sometimes struggle with a loss of identity. It has been my experience that women tend to disassociate from their feelings more readily than men. A woman can appear normal and be intelligent but feel empty. This emptiness sometimes translates into a need to avoid one's own feelings and focus on someone else's issues. This loss of personal identity can impair relationships. It can have negative consequences for the enabler because even if you witness poor behavior or debilitating behavior in someone that you care about, there is a tendency to overlook or validate and come to the rescue of the person who is struggling in an attempt to hide the real issue, which is with you. If left unaddressed and unresolved, debilitating behavior for both the enabler and the enabled can lead to even more damaging choices that begin to mimic a war of waging intended good against produced bad. In other words, the initial intentions of helping someone can be good yet how you handle it can produce bad results. Evil precipitated every day behind the prison wall. There was a battle between good and evil all the time and many times evil won. The good appeared in prayer circle and Bible study or when I helped a woman who could not read or write. The evil was more pervasive: cursing, fighting and stealing from one another. This evil occurred almost nonstop, every woman whom I encountered, whether innocent of her present offense or not, had some emotional weakness that landed her in prison – and that included me. It was my observation that most of the women suffered from a lack of personal identity that made it difficult for them to move from a place of self-hatred to spiritual peace for any extended period of time. Most would not admit it, but they hated their image as women.

Women in prison constantly refer to one another as bitch, whether they are in a friendly mood or an angry mood. When one calls the other the B-word, there is either a pleasant response because that reference is acceptable or there is an angry response because of the tone that is being used. I witnessed a lot of anger resting in the souls of my sisters. That rage was a result of a varied amount of complex issues that had touched their lives: sexual abuse, childhood abandonment by parents, drug abuse by mother or father, and the list goes on and on. The women lost their identity in their rage. The emotional bondage that tethered them to their hurt and pain had become so deep that many of them believed they were at a point of no return—so why try to change.

THE DRAMA OF CODEPENDENT WOMEN IN PRISON

My interaction with traumatized "birds" continued when I arrived at Edna Mahan Correctional Facility the state prison for women.

FILLING THE VOID

The interesting concept about this whole notion of enabling is that enablers and the enabled seem to feed off one another. Each is dependent on the other for fulfilling some unmet need. A classic example involves the mother who has suffered years of abuse. She has been beaten, verbally abused, demeaned, and dishonored. The woman has heard it over and over again that she is nothing, and she begins to feel like nothing and resigns herself to the fact that she is nothing. She never really will be able to find healthy relationships with people of the opposite sex; she is abused but keeps going back for more. There is a void in her life which she desperately needs filled. The woman keeps returning to the same abusive relation-ship. She can't stop. She needs to feel love, and somewhere in her warped sense of thinking, any attention—whether abusive or not—is enough to show that she matters in this world.

This translates into the woman investing her time and energy in trying to rescue someone who does not want to be rescued. This conduct gives her a false sense of self-worth and confidence in her abilities. She continues in this course of conduct typically with a loved one who is either addicted to drugs or alcohol. Slowly but consistently, she overlooks the faults in the person and supplies what she thinks the other person needs, which is usually to be rescued by her. The enabled person falls and the woman picks them back up; they fall again, and she picks them up again. She keeps going back for more because they need her. A woman who enables has not even realized that she has become an enabler who is feeding off the enabled. She is starved for the feeling of importance and power she feels when she comes to the aid of the broken person. She is filling the void in her life that was hollowed out by abuse suffered over years.

Here is what's crazy: The enabled person is feeding off of the enabler as well. A person cannot be enabled unless another person permits the behavior. The enabled drug addict, alcoholic, and irresponsible person have nowhere to turn if the enablers in their lives are not there to direct them when they fall off course. I witnessed this firsthand while incarcerated.

DIABLO'S DISRESPECT

I have shared many stories of the women whom I met in prison who were both enabled and enablers. One of the most devastating I encountered was the story of fifteen year old Diablo, who was serving time for murder because she took the wrap for her boyfriend who actually killed someone. She lacked any positive image of herself, was enabled by her family and ultimately validated destructive behavior of others.

Diablo was loud, fearless and wrong most of the time. She disrespected everyone including herself. I approached her one day to see if she would talk to me. Maybe I should have been afraid because she was in for murder, but I wasn't.

Diablo said she was the victim of sexual abuse by her father. She told her mother, but her mother did not believe her and did not care. She turned to the wrong crowd for comfort. In and out of Juvenile detention, the fifteen year sentence for murder in state prison was the longest she ever received. Grandma enabled Diablo by making excuses for her behavior, blaming it on Diablo's father for abusing her. While there was merit to why Diablo acted out, Grandma's response to the behavior presented the problem: Diablo was enabled.

THE SELLING OF EVE

Codependent relationships center on the need to feel significant by each party. Eve was a pretty Hispanic girl, twenty-seven years of age. Eve was doing time for prostitution. Her bunk was directly in front of the day room. When we talked, she told me that she had a bad drug addiction which forced her into the streets. She really believed that her boyfriend was her savior because, as she put it, he took care of her and gave her everything that she needed. I asked her what that meant, and she said he brought her drugs, supplied her clothes and gave her a place to live. Basically, he enabled her. Her repayment to her boyfriend, who was also a drug addict, was to prostitute herself. She sold her body and gave him the money to continue on the crazy path that he chose. Both Eve and her boyfriend latched on to a relationship because of need. Eve felt needed by her pimp boyfriend so she prostituted herself. Her boyfriend felt significant because he believed he was taking care of Eve. Both latched on to a negative reality in the relationship.

GREEN LIGHT, RED LIGHT, YELLOW LIGHT

When considering ways to avoid enabling, stopping and thinking about your behavior is important. One day in the cafeteria three women started fights. One attacked the other over her "girlfriend," and the girlfriend jumped in to protect her new mate. All three of the women were arrested and put in Lock, which is solitary confinement. As described to me, it is a small 10x10 room with a metal non-seat toilet and a tiny sink. In Lock, you don't shower; you wear the same clothes every day. One of the women in the fight had just been classified to Grounds, which is the general population and minimal security. The other one had been released to Grounds three months earlier. I was amazed at how quickly these women were willing to give up their privileges based on their emotions. On the other hand, our emotions act as signals in our life, directing us in both positive and negative ways.

I have termed the signal analogy "green light, red light, yellow light." If you move too fast when the light turns green, you are at risk of serious injury, which is either self-inflicted or caused by another. The red light emotion may keep you stagnated and unable to think or move at all. It is the yellow light emotion that gives you an opportunity to proceed through life's circumstances with caution. If I had yielded to the yellow light, I am certain I would not have landed in prison. I would have thought more carefully and intentionally about my moves concerning my family and undoubtedly I would have taken a different direction.

The women involved in the fights over the past two days flew when the light turned green. They did not think. They did not stop. They just proceeded into a major intersection of confusion without caution, and a collision occurred. All three have now suffered harm and if they do not begin to understand their behaviors, the harm will be irreparable.

Living in a place where people are destroyed because of their pain and reliance on other people brings to glaring light the issue of codependency. During my time of incarceration, I witnessed many mother/daughter drug scenarios. The mothers used drugs with their daughters, and some of them were incarcerated with their daughters. The use of drugs was the common denominator, and more times than not the daughters were using because they could not handle the emotional rejection and depravation by their drug-addicted mothers. The mothers felt guilty because they knew their drug addiction had contributed to, if not caused, the addictions of their daughters. As I witnessed the behavior and heard the stories of these incarcerated families, I kept asking myself: Where do I fit in? Was I there to help myself or to help the other women who were overcome with pain? I really felt it was a little of both. By helping the women, I thought about my own actions and what I needed to change in order to defeat my own enabling behavior.

REFLECTION EXERCISES:
CHAPTER FOUR

Name the people in your life with weaknesses that you nurture and take care of.

_____

_____

_____

How does it make you feel to take care of a person who should be taking care of themselves?

_____

_____

_____

Do you look for validation from other people?

_____

_____

_____

As a child did you have responsibilities that should have been handled by an adult?

_____

_____

_____

Describe yourself. Write down your good and bad qualities. Is there anything you would like to change?

_____

_____

_____

Write down the names of the people who are closest to you. When was the last time you heard, "I love you" from that person and how often do you hear it?

_____

_____

_____

What is your image of a strong person? Do you possess all or some of those qualities?

_____

_____

_____

Chapter Five
ETHICS AND ENABLING

"When you start compromising yourself and your morals for the people around you, it's probably time to change the people around you."
-Unknown

IN ALL OF my research on the topic of codependency and enabling, I did not find one discussion on ethical dilemmas apparent in the lives of enablers. I have no graphs or statistics to share. What I do have is my belief based upon my personal experience and understanding of the definition of ethical dilemmas. I think we all know when we cross the ethical line; whether we want to admit it or not, is another story.

WHO WAS I?

With everything that occurred during those four calamitous years in my life and the attention it attracted, I had to ask myself the question: Who was I? The big issue for the prosecutor and judge was that I had breached the public trust, hence an ethical lapse. The newspapers, politicians, and prosecutors painted a picture of a ruthless, cruel opportunist who did a disservice to the citizens of the State of New Jersey and, therefore, deserved to be locked up for several years. After all, I was entrusted with a position of power and influence and I had abused it. They did not believe that my actions warranted a second chance. In fact, they thought that my actions were so severe that they were unforgivable prompting the prosecutors to ask the judge to sentence me to seven years in prison (to help put this in perspective, in some cases, there are murderers who do not receive such a stiff seven-year sentence).

During those dark days when I looked in the mirror, I saw the physical me, an African American woman in her late forties who had grown up in poverty and dysfunction but despite the obstacles accomplished many positive things in her life. When I looked at the pictures of my family, I saw a wife who loved her husband; a mother who loved her children; a daughter, sister, and aunty who loved her family. I thought that the most important thing about me was that I had raised two wonderful sons who were in college, and up until my incarceration, I was raising an eleven year-old-son. I never missed a basketball game, swim meet, football or soccer game that my sons participated in. As a matter of fact, I never missed anything that involved my children because I always signed them up and along with my husband, chauffeured them to their activities.

When the incident came to light in 2004, I knew that I was in big trouble. After the initial trauma and shock of it all, I began and continued to ask myself during prison who was I? In retrospect, I was a woman who loved the Lord and church, volunteered in various community service activities, worked hard to represent my clients and enjoyed my family, friends, reading, writing and life.

Who was I? I was a woman who, from the moment I entered prison, made a commitment to try and help my sisters, my fellow inmates, by assuring them that no matter what they had done it was possible to start fresh. Who was I? I was an imperfect person; after all, I broke the law and I was in prison dealing with the consequences of my actions. Who was I? A mother who deeply regretted how my actions affected my family, especially my youngest son Isaiah.

Who was I? I was a former lawyer, judge, and ex-public official. Somehow knowing that a few of those titles, which were attached to my name, had ignited a certain perception of me by everyone except me and by the people who really knew me was confusing and disturbing. I was only a judge for thirty days. I was a public official for two years, and an attorney for sixteen. I had never run for political office and rarely associated myself with politics. Three years had passed since the indictment and trial, and it all seemed like a short time in my now 49 years of life, compared to how long I have been a daughter, sister, wife, mother, and friend to many.

Self-reflection was difficult for me to tackle because it spoke to the core of who I thought I was. More importantly, when I began to understand the behavior of an enabler, it touched on the lengths that an enabler would go, right or wrong, in order to protect someone they loved with no thought of consequences for themselves – like total exhaustion, stress, anger, and emptiness.

THE MORAL EROSION

You may question what this has to do with enabling. EVERYTHING! The image of a controlling, angry, sad, empty person is deeply associated with the characteristics and behavior of an enabler. Normally, enablers seem in healthy control but carry around a lot of deadly weight. With all of the issues, it is not surprising that there is an eroding of the moral compass. In many respects, enablers are living a lie which they hope no one ever discovers. Morals are concerned with judgment of goodness or badness of human action or character and with principles or rules of right and wrong conduct. The very people who enablers engage are acting in wrong conduct, and enablers know it but choose to overlook it in order to further their agenda of control and dominance or their need to feel loved and significant.

While I engaged in this course of conduct, some of what I had become was evident to me, but why I had become this person was still buried in my subconscious. The reality is that, as an enabler, you are more inclined to take risks that are detrimental and not think about the consequences, or if you do dwell on your conduct it is easily justifiable. I accept responsibility for handling the hiring of my sister and mother the wrong way, thus I have to accept that my moral compass was off. I did not weigh the risk of how my choice could harm them or anyone else. I never even thought about it. I did not believe I was breaking any law, and in any arena outside the public official area, I probably would have just been fired. But as I sat many months in prison and considered the course of events, there would probably not be a story to tell if I were just fired. I would not have been forced to consider anything about my actions concerning this topic, and I would not be in a position to help people as I am trying to do with the writing of this book.

THE SHADOWS

Not everything is black and white. Sometimes the most difficult challenges remain in the shadows between the two. The challenge that most people face when dealing with ethical issues is not the obvious ethical lapses, like not being truthful about your education or lying on an application, which is pretty clear cut. The question of ethics becomes murky when decisions fall in the shadows. For example, if your son is an alcoholic and he arrives home drunk unable to get up and go to work the next day, do you call his job and make excuses for him, lie and say he's sick and can't make it in? Well, he is hung over, and alcoholism could be considered an illness. However, you as the enabler are complicit in covering up the real problem: you have an alcoholic for a son.

Another example might be that you have been the victim of

spousal abuse, and one day you are out with friends, who notice a bruise on your face. When questioned, you respond that you fell down a flight of stairs. The truth is you were pushed. The abuser is allowed to continue on a course of destruction because you feel the need to protect him. Whether it is out of fear or shame, you are approving the behavior of the enabled.

You could be an employer who repeatedly allows your employee to get away with underperformance while the other employees are working hard; you make excuses for his behavior and overlook his performance by giving the person great employee evaluations. You are not only an enabler, but you are floating in the shadows of right and wrong. It is right to want to help people; it is wrong to turn your head and not be truthful in an attempt to hide the true behavior of a person.

Reversing the roles you are an employee trying to climb the corporate ladder. You find it hard to say no to your boss as he or she hands over work and task that are less than legitimate or at least ethically suspect. Instead of addressing your boss about what you know is wrong you overlook the behavior in an attempt to please him or her.

People would rather not address the shadows of life because it is easier to overlook flaws than to address them. For years, I wandered in the shadows of life because I had reached the pinnacle of my career (at least that is what I believed). I thought that I could not have accomplished all that I had if I was not a good person who had it all together. The reality is that I was a good person; I just did not have it all together. The fact that I was an extremely responsible person is a great characteristic to possess, but the flip side is that my need to uphold my extreme responsible trait meant that I had to project that perception to the world. And in my dealing with the enabled in my life, I was unable to let go of their issues; instead, I took them on as my own.

When a person is seen as taking on someone else's problems in a way that is not irresponsible, that person is generally celebrated for taking the right approach. Subsequently, that person's confidence increases and it affords them the chance to demonstrate their skills of being able to make a notable accomplishment. From their viewpoint and often from the viewpoint of others, this person exudes a spirit of being smart, relatable, adept and forgiving. Each of these admirable traits has a dark side which usually makes well-adjusted people sick and pushes the maladjusted to the shadows areas of life. A desire to showcase their capabilities can place enablers in a position that causes them to over-exaggerate in some areas of their life. Dominance can lend itself to dependency by the enabled. Adaptability can cause the enabler to dance beyond the given boundaries.

The acceptable societal traits that enablers possess may really be less desirable aspects of their enabling personality and have little to do with their good qualities. Enablers have a need to maintain a false image, which is essential in how they view themselves. They are forced to make sacrifices because they cannot deal honestly with whom they are and what their true agenda entails, which is to hide from self. The shadows help to perpetuate their dishonesty when relating to other people because normal exchanges are blocked.

The enabler's profile is extremely complex because there are so many sides, both good and bad, on which to hang one's hat. Shadows allow enablers to walk on both sides of the fence without the suspicion of being an outright liar. After all, they are only acting to protect the enabled, right?

Do You Believe What You See?

Self-discovery for me took a lot of time and many months of critical reflection. Looking in the mirror, I realized that I had fought hard to escape a life which I thought was unhealthy, but I never really dealt with my past. I brought a lot of baggage into the new world that I had created for myself. My insecurities about not being good enough, my shame and embarrassment regarding my father, my anger regarding my family life (why were we not living like the Leave it to Beaver family), my need to control everything in my life and others because I had no control as a child, my lack of trust, my denial about my past, and my weak boundaries. Wow! There was a lot to admit, but it was who I had become and I needed to hear it from me.

As you read this book, consider your own life and the possibility that you are an enabler and that being so is a detriment to you and a detriment to the one you are enabling. I believe that everyone has enabled someone at some point in their lives, but it cuts deep when you continue to hurt the person you enable and you hurt yourself in the process. Looking in the mirror to search out your demons can be difficult. Enablers tend to avoid mirrors because the focus is not really supposed to be on you. You gain your power by pouring into others which leaves you little time to focus on yourself. The reflection of an enabler is usually marred with unhappiness about your childhood, family, relationships or marriage. Your anger is evident in how you relate to people, especially the one you are enabling; you have a tendency to lash out because of the frustration you feel toward that person. This anger repeats itself in other relationships, affecting possibly your productivity and how you deal with your co-workers or employees. Have you ever snapped at someone for no reason at all or at least not the reason that generated your behavior? Your mind is on your problem, which is usually the person you are enabling, but your anger is directed toward another. I believe this is termed displaced aggression.

Looking in the mirror requires you to beat yourself up, scream, yell and shed tears concerning your behavior. You may even have to break the mirror and replace it with another one once you have figured out who you want to be going forward.

Dee was my best friend in prison, if you can really have a best friend in prison. We spent many months together talking about who she was and who she wanted to be. Dee had been adopted as a child and never really dealt with that in a healthy way. She started using drugs early and then became a drug dealer. She had a daughter who she raised while she was on the streets and who was then raised by her cousin when Dee was in jail. Dee's daughter grew up watching and learning the life of her mother. She too eventually landed in jail. At one point, they were both in jail at the same time. Dee had been enabled by relatives and so had her daughter. During our time together, Dee talked about wanting a different life.

One day standing in front of Plexiglas (no real mirrors were allowed in jail), I asked Dee to look at herself and tell me what she saw. She was not happy with what she discovered. "I hate me," she said.

I responded, "What do you hate about yourself?"

"I hate that I used drugs. I hate that I sold drugs. I hate that I prostituted myself. I hate that I stole. I hate that I lied. I hate that I deprived my daughter of a life with a responsible mother." Dee looked in the mirror and saw a self-destructive person. How was she to move past her demons?

Although my demons were not the same as Dee's, we still had work to do on ourselves. I told her that she had taken the first step which was looking in the mirror and affirming out loud what she had become and why.

As an enabler, you cannot get past who you have become unless you deal with who you are in the present. The ugliness of your life has to be spoken out loud. You may have to use bad language and curse yourself. I remember on many days after the indictment and during the course of the investigation and trial, looking at myself in the mirror and yelling, "Stupid, stupid, stupid." I knew everyone else thought I was stupid and I was, but I needed to own my stupidity. There is no opportunity for you to start healing as an enabler unless you agree to become critical about your actions and what they have done to your life. As far as addressing the enabler in your life, that cannot be accomplished until you deal with you.

The mirror can be an intimidating experience because you are basically afraid to look inside of you and see anything negative even if you know it exists. The mirror can also be a transformative place if you are willing to take a hard look at yourself with total acceptance of your faults and the willingness to make the changes necessary to redefine who you have become.

I challenge you to look in the mirror. Yes, I mean a real mirror in your home and see if what you are looking at is something that you can live with. If it is, then either you are okay or you are in denial and not ready to do the work necessary for transformation. If you find that it is difficult to look at yourself because you don't like what you see then you have taken the first step which is acceptance.

Ethical lapses move you away from your moral compass, and once you have travelled that road and been exposed, it is difficult to recover. People can forgive drug addiction, prostitution, alcoholism, but when you have been made out to be a person unworthy of belief, it is a tough and long road to perdition. Prior to my legal troubles, I was well respected as both an attorney and a professional. I was recognized for my work in the legal profession and often asked to participate in many worthwhile events. During my legal battle, I was portrayed as a terrible person who lived my entire life breaking the law. Upon my emergence back into society having accepted responsibility for my actions and repaid my debt, for some people I am forever under a cloak of suspicion regarding my ethics. My credibility is often questioned in silence because people are long on memory and short on forgiveness. My prior work and accomplishments seem a distant memory because of one mistake. As major as the mistake was, it resulted out of my need to be all things to all people, which is impossible. The reality is that you have to pick yourself up and keep going, not for the sake of what other people think of you, but most important because of what you think of you.

Enablers, it is time for you to get honest with yourself. I want you to understand the gravity of your offense as an enabler. Some things cause irreparable harm. Your actions are hurting the one you love, digging that person deeper in a ditch at the same time that you are self-destructing – all without even knowing. The saying, "To err is human, to forgive divine" may not be applicable when you have caused a multitude of pain by crossing the ethical line, shifting your moral compass, wading into the gray areas, and refusing to look in the mirror.

REFLECTION EXERCISES:
CHAPTER FIVE

Take a look at yourself in a mirror. Do you like what you see on the outside? What about the inside?

_____

_____

_____

Do you ever take the time to reflect on your attitude or behavior? Is there anything you would change?

_____

_____

_____

List any rules that you have broken or have almost broken (they do not have to be criminal).For instance, you promise yourself that you will not make excuses for your child's behavior (e.g. dropped out of school and won't get a job).

_____

_____

_____

Chapter Six
SYSTEMIC ENABLING

"Most people are as happy as their self-confidence will allow them to be."
-Shannon L. Adler

DURING MY TIME of incarceration it became clear to me that the interactions between the CO's (corrections officers) and the inmates are evidence of a broken system which perpetuates codependent behavior. Again I have no statistical data to share with you regarding my claim. I do have pragmatic knowledge based upon my personal experience and observations. While punishment is the main objective of all penal institutions, humiliation, abuse, tearing down of self-esteem and disrespect overshadowed the goal of deterrence. The attitudes and actions of the CO's in the prison I witnessed were controlling and abusive with every attempt to make the women feel as if they could never turn their lives around and become productive citizens in society.

Based upon my observation of the CO's the prison system is just as guilty of codependent behavior as family members who choose to latch on to dysfunctional relationships with their loved ones out of a need to control. Instead of fostering growth, positive attitudes and life skills with a promise of hope for the future the inmates are made to feel totally dependent on the system. For many of the women, leaving prison and never returning is an anomaly because the Department of Corrections has no real advantage in making sure that the women are prepared to return to society and contribute in a meaningful way. Recidivism is the hidden objective. Without repeat offenders there would be no jobs for the CO's. Other businesses stand to lose money as well, such as the counselors, independent contractors doing business with the prison and administrators to name a few. It is better to encourage bad behavior among the inmates to insure that they stand a high probability in returning. The intuitions need the prisoners and some prisoners feel they need the security of the prison. Through the relationship of the COs' and the prisoners the two meet one another's needs in a dysfunctional way.

The negative interaction between the correction officers and inmates were numerous and consistent. CO Wallen was a troubled soul. One night while I was still in MCCC, I held Bible study a little later than usual because CO Wallen handed out hair supplies and, of course, most of the women wanted to do their hair immediately. CO Wallen was an interesting but predictable woman. She had personal issues relating to her husband, who was a police officer. Several of the women on the tier were prostitutes and admitted meeting CO Wallen's husband on a professional basis in the street. CO Wallen was insecure and vindictive. She obviously had no control or power in her home and suffered from her own pain of disrespect by her husband so she chose to act out her control issues while at work. The biggest problem was her attitude. She treated the women as if they were less than human by cursing at them, threatening them, calling them names. Unfortunately her conduct re-enforced the negative perception of self-worth that each woman inmate carried.

On the night of Bible study, CO Wallen sent Wanda, the runner (a runner is a person assigned to run errands or do dirty work for the CO and perceived as a badge of honor), to take the chairs from us. We had no choice but to give them up, but surprisingly, the ladies remained by my bed and stood as we finished our study. Her actions were without merit and intentional just to disturb what was occurring in Bible study. Wallen, like many of the other CO's did not want the women to strengthen themselves with positive reinforcement.

I have no idea what the training of the COs' entails, but I suspect it has nothing to do with lifting the women emotionally. During my stay at Edna Mahan CO Williams was pathetic. From the time she hit the doors at 6:00 a.m., she yelled, screamed, threatened, degraded, humiliated, cursed, and demeaned the women. She felt totally empowered in her position and fed off of confrontation. Sounds like an enabler characteristic. It appeared that she enjoyed it when the women responded to her antics because, in that environment, she had the last word. She often referred to the women as idiots. I am convinced she had control issues while being totally self-absorbed. Her insults were never-ending. She called us mindless and went out of her way to make the women feel stupid.

The stories of control, disrespect and abuse carried from one institution to the next, and are too numerous to share. What I do want to share is a word of reproach for the CO's. Instead of tearing incarcerated women down, why not use the opportunity to mentor them through your words actions and deeds. I understand the need for separation; however, if you can laugh with them about the antics and crimes committed in the streets there is also time for you to encourage them not to return to prison.

Women inmates do not accept the negative characterizations that are placed on you. There may not be the opportunity to disagree with the CO's; after all, you are under their physical control, but you can tune out anything that is not positive and focus on the good that you can do once you are free. With the blessing of the Lord, you control your destiny. The CO's do not.

REFLECTION EXERCISE:
CHAPTER SIX

Have you ever found yourself in an abusive and controlling relationship with you as the victim? Was it verbal or physical? Did you leave or did you stay? If you stayed why?

_____

_____

_____

Have you ever felt emotionally stuck? What caused it? Have you been able to overcome the feeling?

_____

_____

_____

Part Two
Resolutions

Chapter Seven
THE AWAKENING

"Anyone can hide. Facing up to things, working through them,
that's what makes you strong."
-Sarah Dessen

GOING TO PRISON is obviously an eye opener; the assumption is something went terribly wrong in a person's life. Without realizing it at the time some of my darkest days actually occurred before I was indicted or went to prison, days when I was under immense pressure from my job and family. I was the pro bono (that means free) attorney for my church and pastor, assisting with legal matters. I had a private practice which I found stressful because of the great responsibility I felt for my clients. When the opportunity presented itself to fill the chief of staff position for the Commerce Commission, I was ready to make a move from self-employment to a steady paycheck. I closed my practice and headed to Trenton. Once settling into the new position, I assumed more responsibility than I was prepared for. I felt an enormous amount of self-inflicted pressure to please my boss. I never said no to any requests. I said self-inflicted because of my control issues. No was not an option. I did not think there was anything that I could not handle. After the indictment I was forced to resign and the only job I could find was working in a Subway sandwich shop for a friend who eventually let me go.

I loved to read and finally had time. I picked up every self-help book I could find, saturating myself with the words of inspiration, empowerment and hope. I also began to journal, which I still do and find extremely cathartic. I began to realize that with all of my success I had lived a part of my life by living for others. I lived through Shawn's issues and made them my own. I lived through Candace's traumas and made them my own. I lived through Mommy and Daddy's issues and made them my own. Even as an attorney my clients' issues became mine. My life was their life. I had become a crutch for everyone, and it had not really bothered me because I believed it was what I was supposed to do.

During this time, I also sought therapy. Well, actually therapy sought me. One morning the telephone rang. The answering machine picked up (I had stopped answering the phone because of the constant calls from the media), and there was a woman's voice. She introduced herself as a professional therapist who read about my problems in the newspaper and was calling to offer her services. She stressed that she had no agenda, except to help another woman out. She offered her services and told me not to worry about money. If I ever wanted to talk, she would make herself available. My initial thought was absolutely not. I did not trust anyone because people were turning against me left and right and others dropped me like a hot potato. Besides, I was not ready to talk.

The shame, guilt, and intense pressure of not knowing what the future held kept me up many nights. One sleepless night I lay in a fetal position on my bedroom floor begging God to take my pain away. I was a church-going Christian, and I loved the Lord. While I thanked God for my abilities, I was sure God was not pleased with me at this particular time in my life. Through my tears and in my prayers, I suddenly had a strong desire to live and to seek help. The next morning, I called the therapist and scheduled my first appointment. During my first visit, I cried for the entire hour. Dr. Debbie sat quietly letting me pour out everything I had held in. Over the next few months, I opened up about my life, my family, my joys, and my pain.

I spent a year in therapy with Dr. Debbie unpacking my issues and as a result of the culmination of help that I sought through prayer, reading the Bible, self-help books and self-reflection, my awakening began. I realized that my hopes, dreams, successes, and failures were marred by the dark side of enabling, which had become a part of me. Just as I had taken on everyone's issues and handled them, I was determined to be victorious in tackling the enabling bondage that captivated me.

I really wanted to understand how I could love my family, hear about their problems, but live my life taking care of me and allowing them to take care of themselves. There were not many books on the market. Self-care author Melody Beattie wrote Codependent No More, and Angelyn Miller wrote a booked called The Enabler. I give both books credit for tackling this tough issue in a positive way. As I began to write about my own journey, I realized that there were still questions that I needed answered and that might shed light on others as they tackle the same issue. As a rehabilitated enabler professing to be fully delivered from the grip of enabling, I wanted to share what has helped me to finally be set free.

WHOSE RESPONSIBILITY IS IT?

As I pulled back the many layers of sadness, responsibility, adversity, and dysfunction in my life, I started with the question: Whose responsibility is it? With my mother out of the home working and my father out of reality addicted to drugs, I really believed that taking care of Shawn and Candy was my responsibility. I shared this with my therapist, and she responded. "But you were a child doing adult things."

Although therapy is not for everyone, it did help me. Ultimately, it was up to me to take action to do the work necessary to change my thinking and actions as it related to enabling others. I truly believe that there are steps that persons can take on their own to win the battle against codependency and enabling. This is why I wrote the book. I share my therapy session in line with my promise of transparency in hopes to provide one of several alternatives for defeating codependency.

Mom attended one of my sessions. I looked her in the eyes with a bit of trepidation and asked, "Mommy, why did you expect so much of me?"

She said, "Because I thought you could handle it." Wow! I did not know how to respond verbally, so I just cried. I had always exhibited confidence, intelligence and maturity from a very young age. I don't think mommy was wrong in her assessment because of how I carried myself, even as a child. She really believed that, as a child, I could handle the pressures of a juvenile delinquent brother, an immature sister and a drug addict father. The crazy thing is that I thought I was supposed to handle it and did not see anything I did as a problem when it was occurring.

Mommy's life as a child and adult had its share of adversity. I knew it. I held no animosity toward her. She has always been proud of me. She encouraged, supported and loved me. With my brother's emotional issues, my sister as the baby and my father who was lost, I was her strong support -- the one she could count on. She believed in me as her child and that was not an entirely bad thing when I consider all of the women in prison who had no one to believe in them.

With the many layers of adversity and sadness in my life, I end with the question: Does my mother realize that her encouragement and love for me as a child helps me to cope with my issues of enabling today? Taking care of Shawn and Candy was my responsibility. Although I was a child doing adult things, today, as an adult, my inner child's truth resonates in me. I am blessed to have a mother who "thought I could handle it" as she truly believed in me, and for that, I am thankful.

If you are enabling any person in your life, understand that you really do not have to be your brother's keeper. This is a biblical association referring to Cain and Abel and that Cain killed his brother over what theologians have suggested is jealousy. However, the analogy is used today to question our responsibilities to others. I say that as family you have a responsibility to care for one another, but that does not mean it is ever at your own expense. So, to answer the question as an enabler, am I my brother's, sister's, mother's, or father's keeper? The answer is a resounding NO.

Recognition of your situation is important. Look at your family cycle and your childhood and decide if you were placed in a position of unpreparedness as a caretaker. If this is your reality, address the person or persons who placed you in this situation. I don't mean in a hostile manner but as a matter of beginning your healing. To defeat the antagonist, you have to face the point where you push responsibility over its healthy edge. You need to understand how you became the person you are. The antagonist is not my mother; or the person who pushed you, it is the enabling spirit we possess and have to face in order to heal.

TAKING OWNERSHIP

The next critical step in preparing to battle with your enabling spirit is to take ownership over it. Okay, so maybe my life would have been different if I had not learned how to enable, but the fact remains that I did learn how to enable and I was an enabler. I had to own that title, whether I liked it or not. When you remain in denial about the things that have held you in bondage, you can't move forward. Denying that you are an enabler means that your behavior will remain consistent. Like a drug addict or an alcoholic, every time they take a drug or drink they want more and live for the next opportunity to succumb to their desire. This might sound extreme to you, but is it? Your need, your drug, is to fix people and to make excuses for doing so. You feel a certain amount of satisfaction when you exhibit your Messiah complex over someone else's life. This behavior does not stop after one "fix." You wait until the next time you are needed and begin the process all over again.

Deal with the Demon

Deal with the demons of enabling; don't run from them. Running from your problem will only exhaust you. You have heard the expression: you can run but you sure can't hide. This is true of any situation that you find yourself in which requires you to face ugly truths about yourself. It always seems easier to act like your problem does not exist as opposed to facing it head on. The tendency to avoid internal confrontation is appealing, but it never works. Take, for instance, the alcoholic who believes that the best way to stop drinking is to move to another town away from his favorite liquor store. He failed to realize that the next town has liquor stores, too. If he does not address what has led him to drink in his life, he will soon find another favorite liquor store.

Today is the day that you can be honest with yourself and admit that you have a problem. This really is your first step. My last stop before I was released was the Fenwick House, a residential drug treatment halfway house for women. I did not suffer from drug addiction. This, however, was the only place the corrections officials could send me since the other halfway house was not a fit. A condition of the program was attendance at Narcotics Anonymous. I attended twice week. At the beginning of each meeting everyone, except me, introduced themselves the same way, "Hi, my name is Claudia, and I am a drug addict." I was excused from making the statement. Looking back, I understand that the meeting could not begin until each person acknowledged their demon, which meant they were taking ownership for who they had become.

You cannot defeat an invisible adversary; you are shooting blind. By acknowledging the demons in your life, you put a face on the problem and place yourself in a much better position to begin your line of attack. Whether you are an enabler, or have been enabled, or wear both hats, the work toward recovery begins on the inside. Don't be afraid of what you discover about yourself. If you are like me, some of it will not be pretty, but if you want real change to occur, pretty is of no consequence. It is the ugly inside that needs to surface.

REFLECTION EXERCISE:
CHAPTER SEVEN

Write a list of things that you do to strengthen yourself emotionally.

_____

_____

_____

How do you handle pressure from family, friends and co-workers?

_____

_____

_____

Are you willing to share your feelings about being overwhelmed with people outside of your family?

_____

_____

_____

Do you think talking about the pressures of life will help you?

_____

_____

_____

Write a list of the people that you feel are your responsibility to care for (e.g. emotionally, physically, and monetarily) and reflect on whether they could make it through life without you. Furthermore, can you make it through life without feeling responsible for taking care of these people?

_____

_____

_____

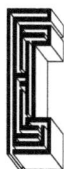

Chapter Eight
BREAKTHROUGHS

*"Every challenge you encounter in life is a fork in the road.
You have the choice to choose which way to go."*
-Ifeanyi Enoch Onuoha

THE FOUL LINE

THE HARDEST THING for me to do was to set boundaries when it came to my personal life. The foul line is a good place, if you are aiming in the right direction, but it can be a bad place, if you keep missing the mark.

Aiming in the right direction requires practice. You have to keep your eye in the direction that you want your own life to go. This seems easy: You have a goal, you see it in your mind, and then you aim for it. The problem arises when interference gets in the way. If you allow the distractions from other people and their situations to disturb your focus, then you will miss your mark. The good news is that you can try again and again until you get it right, but eventually you have to get it right.

Enablers have to practice, practice, practice, when it comes to not enabling others. The women in the state prison ranged from drug addicts and thieves to murderers. Even though I was surrounded by women with violent pasts, I never felt afraid. I believed my purpose was bigger than me. I needed to see the effects of crossing the foul line in the lives of the other women, and I needed to feel the devastation of not just being on the foul line but crossing it.

Twice a week, the visiting hall at Edna Mahan was full of the enabled and enablers. Family members travelled from all over the state to stand in a long line with small children and strangers to go through security; to get patted down by rude, disrespectful guards who considered the visitors just as bad as the inmates; to sit in a room for two hours while guards walked around and listened to their conversations. The families went to prison and became prisoners every time they visited an inmate. They could not leave before the end of the visits, and they could not have physical contact with the inmates.

Is it wrong for you to visit your loved one if she has to go to prison? Not really, but if your visits are a result of years of the same behavior, that may mean you have condoned her problem and you are continuing to contribute to her problem. I met so many women who said this was their fourth, fifth, even sixth time returning to prison. I was in disbelief because I could not grasp that I was in prison one time. The repeat offenders are the best example of the enabled continuing on a course of conduct and not knowing how to stop, and of enablers not knowing how to stop giving help. There was no tough love for these women. These were the very same women who received weekly visits from family and friends. Many of the ladies shared with me that the men and women coming to visit them were the same people who had mistreated them, lied to them, and stole from them while on the street. The enablers—a.k.a. repeat offenders—who regularly visited the inmates had no practice in learning not to enable. I would go out on a limb and say most had no idea that they were enabling.

No is a Complete Sentence

The hardest thing for most people to do is to change a course of conduct that they are used to and want to continue. It takes practice. What if the habitual enablers who routinely visited an inmate who was there for their third, fourth, or fifth time, stopped visiting? What if you said no to the person in your life that has shown repeated self-destructive behavior? You have the right to say no, even if it is to someone you love. No does not mean that you have let the person down; it may mean that you have picked them up and saved their life.

If you have been enabling someone for a long period of time, the first no will be the hardest. You realize that saying no is what has to be done in the situation, but you really want to say yes. So, the next time you are faced with a situation where you should say no, you give in and say yes. You experience a wave of emotions regarding your ability to say no to the person who needs to hear no the most.

When you fall off of the wagon with your no response, get back up, dust yourself off, and when the next opportunity comes for you to say no to the person you are enabling, SAY NO! The more you say no to the enabled, the easier it becomes.

The other benefit of saying no to the person you are enabling is that you begin the process of healing as an enabler. Every time you say no to bad behavior or you cease to rescue a person from self-destructive behavior, you move further and further away from your own crippling behavior, which is enabling others.

You must tell yourself that no needs to be said in the relationship. It takes practice. So don't fear the foul line. Use it to strengthen yourself and to help your loved ones. If you find yourself unable to say no without the feelings of guilt and helplessness for people in your space, then there are other alternatives, which may be needed to deliver you from the grip of enabling.

SELF-DETACHMENT VS. DETACHMENT

Detachment is difficult when the person you are trying to detach yourself from is you. Yes, you, detaching from the desire to control others, to fix others and rescue others. The most talked about break-through in relation to an enabler is detaching from the enabled. Let's talk about what self-detachment is. My definition of self-detachment is the ability of a person to remove parts of their character that are detrimental to the whole being. Ability, removal, and detriment are the operative words in defining self-detachment.

Your ability is power driven. You have to come to the realization that you have the power to change situations in your life that are not good for you. When you think about the emotional and physical effects of remaining attached to a negative person or situation, you are probably unhappy more times than you are happy. This is a realization which should cause you to want to make a shift in your own conduct and reactions to situations that ultimately negatively impact your life.

Removal is taking away the unhealthy things that presently occupy your emotional space. The space inside of you is filled with strengths and weaknesses. In the case of an enabler, your strengths in one area can be a major weakness in another. For example, in order for you to operate as a good leader or as the go-to person in times of trouble, people must see you as a responsible person who can take charge of a situation and find a remedy—that is a strength. In your role as the enabler, you normally step into situations with the intent of taking charge of a person's life and the situation. The problem is that the person you are leading is really leading you down a path of self-destruction because you do not know how to stop what you are doing and instead, let the person figure it out on his or her own. This is about your space and what you possess inside, not the other person. You have to get out of your own head and stop believing that you are the fixer. You can't fix everything and you can't fix other people. Your role is to support in a way that it does not take away from who you are.

Detriment is the last word of the definition which makes up self-detachment. In the medical profession, the doctor's oath is "first do no harm." My thought is first do no harm to yourself. As an enabler, it is to your detriment every time you excuse wrong behavior and try to fix someone else. Each time, you are harming yourself just like you are harming the enabled. You have to always keep in the forefront of your mind the harm that it causes you when you fail to say no—harm in the sense that you are so engrossed in someone else's life that you lose sight of your own. Your frustration with the individual and the situations causes you to remain in a constant state of anger and resentment. You cross lines, make excuses, and even lie to remain in control of the enabled. These actions harm you just as much as they harm the enabled. You have to remove your own bad behavior so that, ultimately, you do not hurt yourself.

MY OWN WORST ENEMY

Sometimes we can be our own worst enemy. During the years of my enabling, I took on the role of public enemy number one to myself. Self-detachment had been a constant struggle for me. First, it was with my sister, brother, and mother. The entire Commerce incident, which led to my indictment and subsequent imprisonment, was because of my inability to self-detach from my own personal weaknesses. There was always something inside of me that said I can handle every situation and I do not need advice or help from others. I associate this character flaw with my need to control, not my ability to handle a situation or crisis. My need to control was my weakness.

A need to control people or situations correlates to lack of something required. Over the years I constantly questioned myself.

What was I lacking in my own personality that caused me to make such a terrible misstep? One of the issues I identified was my relationship with my father and what I witnessed in his behavior had a devastating effect on me emotionally. Why I did not realize this at an earlier point in my life when things were going well I cannot explain, except to say that normally it is personal tragedy, adversity, or failure that causes people to look at their own behavior and actions, to reflect, and perhaps come to terms with where they went wrong.

I believe I shifted into overdrive wanting desperately not to succumb to the weaknesses that plagued my father. I had witnessed his drug addiction, and every member of my family had become affected by it. I knew I did not want my life to take the turn that it took for my father, so I just kept moving in another direction. However, what I did not realize is that, as I moved, I took a lot of junk with me. Anger and sadness were at the top of the list. I truly was angry at my dad for being so weak. The other side of my emotion was sadness. I wanted a different father, the kind I saw on television, with the briefcase who always hugged his children and gave them nurturing advice.

Armed with all of this baggage, I walked into my adult years confident that my life would be different than the one I knew as a child. I took charge of my life and through education tried to make it better. Taking charge of my own life was not a problem; the problem began when I tried to take charge of my family's life. I rolled over all the problems in the family, and everyone looked to me and expected me to handle adverse situations.

The problem with my behavior, as I see it, is that I could not remove (self-detach) my own feelings of anger and sadness, and I thought the remedy for others was me handling their stumbles and living in their dysfunction. I now realize that I first needed to fix myself before I could support anyone else. You notice I said support and not enable; it took a lot for me to grasp the difference, but, thank God, I am now free.

DETACHMENT FROM OTHERS

When experts talk about detachment, they usually mean it in a physical and emotional manner as it relates to someone else. You are in a situation that is negative and unhealthy for you and the best way for you to handle it is to detach yourself from the person who is causing you the discomfort. The American Heritage Dictionary defines detachment as, "the act or process of disconnecting; separation, indifference to the concerns of others, free from emotional involvement."

A word that jumps out is "act" because detachment takes some movement on your part. You have to take the steps to remove yourself from the negative situation. If you find yourself obsessing over someone else's issues, preoccupied or worried about their life and not focusing on your own, STOP! If you obsessively control others' lives and situations as I did, STOP! If you react to every situation that affects someone other than yourself, STOP! If you become the emotional caretaker of others, STOP! You have to make the first move because the enabled person will not. The enabled will not remove themselves. Why should they? They are having all their needs met and their negative conduct validated. You are there every time they fall.

LOVING AND LETTING GO

There were families which detached from some of the ladies on the inside. There were several ladies who did not get visits, cards, or calls. As a result, they were either angry or sad over this revelation.

Delilah was a person dear to me. I loved her as a person who I saw as having a kind heart once she let you in. When I met Delilah, she was serving her fourth or fifth time at Mercer County Correctional Center. Abandoned by her birth mother but adopted by a family and raised in a pretty stable environment, Delilah even had a few years of college behind her. She was tall and pretty thick in stature. Most of the women, if not all, respected her because she was known not to take any mess and could kick butt if she needed to. While Delilah was intimidating to many, I saw her soft spot and was able to pierce through the hardened exterior. We bonded, and that is when I found out about her life. Introduced to drugs by a boyfriend, she became hooked on crack and her life quickly spiraled out of control. I noticed that Delilah did not receive any visits or mail. I asked her about her family, and she said that her mother and father turned their back on her when she started using drugs. Initially, they tried to help her by placing her in rehab, but after the third stint and failure, they decided to detach themselves from the situation and her life. This affected Delilah in many ways—the most obvious was her anger at her family for what she thought was abandonment. Her family, on the other hand, obviously looked at it as detachment. They had to let Delilah go.

That is what detachment is all about—letting go. You have to be strong enough to take a stand against what is destroying you and hurting the person whom you continue to enable. There is a saying: If you love a person, you have to let them go. It does not have to be an unemotional separation laced with a cold and hostile departure; that is not good for you or the person. You can release in the spirit of love. The premise is that the person whom you are enabling is responsible for herself. If there is a problem with that person, you can't solve it; she or he must solve it herself. Her or his problems really are not yours to solve. You have to remove yourself and let that person handle her or his own issues. This may sound cold, but you have to allow a person to be who she or he is, even if at the present time it is destructive for him or her. If you have tried to reach out as a support and the person insists on remaining the same, then you have to consider what the worry and constant engagement is doing to you.

Delilah's family got the memo. Her mother told her that she loved her, but she would not stand by and watch her destroy her life. Unfortunately, her dad died while Delilah was in jail and she did not get a chance to see him or go to the funeral. They removed themselves from the chaos in Delilah's life, realizing that her problem was not theirs to fix. The sad reality is that Delilah is a repeat offender and clearly struggles with maintaining a life absent of drugs and crime. She, like so many other persons who are habitual in their behavior, live in a false reality that they do not need help and that they can control their situation anytime.

In her book Codependent No More, Melody Beattie says detachment is both an act and an art. It is a way of life and a gift that will be given to those who seek it. I like the notion of detachment being a way of life. After my return home from prison, I had to begin a new way of life on so many levels. Still, small issues arose that presented me with a choice of whether I would immerse or extricate myself. My deceased brother's daughter LeLe came to live with me at my request. After years of my niece being shuffled around and growing up in a dysfunctional foster home, I wanted her to have stability in her life. She moved in at the age of eighteen. This was the second time she had lived with me. Prior to this, she lived with me for a year and attended high school, but when I was sentenced to prison, I sent her to California to live with my mother, her grandmother. When she returned to me at age eighteen, her attitude was terrible. She had no respect for my home and little for me. Every day we argued about something, leaving me feeling emotionally drained. I enrolled her into a community college. She underperformed, and I found myself constantly going to the school to try and bail her out with her instructors. I kept excusing her unacceptable behavior and trying to control her situation. I was back to enabling.

This time, though, the red light came on. I realized, after a few months, that I had to let go. Getting up on Sunday morning on my way to church and screaming at the top of my lungs before I left my home was just not good for me. It was time to extricate. One day, my niece was in her room and I asked her to clean the room and then to sit with me so that we could chart out a budget. She refused in her passive-aggressive manner. I had enough. I told her that I would always love her, but it was time for her to leave. She placed her belongings in a plastic bag, and I drove her to a friend's house. Admittedly, because of my enabling characteristics, I was concerned and even thought about letting her back in, but for the first time, my emotions shifted from what was best for her to what was best for me. I needed peace in my home and peace in my spirit.

The difference in my response was a result of my constant prayers, my willingness to accept my own failures, and my desperate desire to stop enabling. Prayer was and continues to be a major force in my life. I surrendered my will to God a long time ago and realized that my strength and determination is directly connected to my prayer life. I am able to work a lot of things out through prayer, talking to God. My faith, believing that He hears and answers, continues to sustain me. I also accepted the fact that I am not perfect and can't fix everyone's problems nor should I want to. Enabling is what got me into the mess with Commerce and landed me in prison, and I really did not ever want to experience that pain again. So I committed to change.

If you are an enabler filled with constant worry, unhappiness, and preoccupation with someone else's life that is spiraling out of control, then it is your time to commit to change. I suggest prayer as the mediator between you and your problem. You really have to take one day at a time, as it is said in AL-Anon (Alcoholics Anonymous), and be honest with yourself, open to change, and willing to take the steps necessary for change. This may mean extricating yourself from the life of someone whom you love, but if you really love them, you will let them go.

REFLECTION EXERCISE:
CHAPTER EIGHT

How easy is it for you to become distracted by other people's issues?

_____

_____

_____

Do you find yourself continuing in a course of conduct that you know is not good for you? What steps have you taken to try and change your reaction?

_____

_____

_____

How often have you said no to the person in your life that needs to hear no?

_____

_____

_____

Why is it so difficult for you to cut the person off if they are causing stress in your life?

_____

_____

_____

How difficult is it for you to detach from others? (detach means to remove yourself emotionally from other people's problems when they cause you stress)

_____

_____

_____

How difficult is it for you to self-detach internally from the things which weigh you down?

_____

_____

This is the "get honest" time for you. (My definition of self-detachment is the ability of a person to remove parts of their character that are detrimental to the whole being.)

_____

_____

_____

Chapter Nine
FALLING IN LOVE WITH ME

*"Learn to love yourself first, instead of loving
the idea of other people loving you."*
-Marc Chernoff

DEPENDING ON WHERE we are emotionally, we are either inclined to
love others and forget about ourselves or love ourselves and be kind
to others in our life. The healthy approach is to love ourselves and
be kind to others. Unfortunately, for the enabler, loving others and
forgetting about ourselves is the rule rather than the exception.

Enablers love their neighbors (people they care about) and hurt
themselves. One reason for this is not feeling good about who you
are. Not liking who you are, much less loving anything about you,
contributes to the self-inflicted hurt.

Enablers are masters at hiding their true feelings. They overcompensate in all areas: from dress to hair to makeup. The reality is that
they continue to inflict pain upon themselves through endless negative thoughts of themselves. They choose to go the extra mile just
to gain acceptance in the world and within their circle of influence.

People who know me find it hard to believe that low self-esteem
had a stronghold on me because I did a good job of masking what
was going on inside. The low self-worth that I sometimes felt was

a result of the dysfunction in my family. I became an overachiever, and my perfect life became a mission. I was under the false belief that perfection meant no errors and no mistakes; failing was not an option. There was always a battle within my family dynamic. I did not think I really fit in with doctors, lawyers, and others who had excelled professionally.

The fall from grace opened my eyes to true self-discovery, acceptance, and action, all of which will help eradicate the confusion brought on by a feeling of low self-worth. Replacing the negative images of yourself helps you begin to understand that a life of perfection is unrealistic and that happiness is obtainable because you are you and not tied up with an image of what you should be.

After being disbarred and losing my license to practice law in two states, I felt like a complete failure because my image was tied up in my title: attorney. Reality hit in a major way when I went to jail and became inmate 601711. I no longer had a name, or an identity; I was relegated to a number. During that time, I realized that who I was did not equate to how many degrees I had or what position I held. I was the same as everyone else. What did matter was how I viewed me and what I wanted for the rest of my life. I decided that I had a lot to offer anyone who wanted to understand the resilience that lives inside all of us. I knew that even if I wanted to portray perfection in my life, it would be difficult to do because of the public nature of my problem. I embraced the reality of my present circumstance, changed what I needed to change, and set out to enrich the lives of others without hurting my own as I had done in the past.

It is a wonderfully liberating feeling to live life feeling good about who I am and not worry about living up to the expectations of others. I realize that I don't have to be perfect, but I do have to be purposeful in my pursuit of my own happiness, never letting someone else's issues take precedence over mine.

As a recovered enabler, I say to all of my cohorts, "Yes, you are and, yes, you can!" You are loving, kind, generous, good-hearted, and caring, and all of these characteristics are acceptable. Think about it, if you did not think about anyone other than yourself, if you were selfish and unconcerned, how could you care so much about another to the point of self-destruction? They are opposing characteristics, unable to coexist in the same mind. Stop beating yourself up for being a good person, but also stop destroying yourself by enabling others. You have to take responsibility over the actions that you perpetuate which cause you harm.

You have a purpose in this life, which does not include being constantly wrapped up in other people's problems. Accept who you are and find your purpose, what God intended you to become. I assure you that the plan God has for your life is not to harm you or to hurt you but to give you a future full of hope. Stop distinguishing yourself from the rest of the world by constantly finding fault with who you are. Everyone makes mistakes in life. People's feelings, though they might differ contextually, are similar, so don't isolate yourself by thinking that you are so different than the rest of humanity.

You deserve the same love that you give. Get rid of the persecution complex that you have lived with most of your life, the idea that everyone is against you or that no one thinks you are worthy. This is not the problem of others; it is your perception problem. This is how you perceive yourself, not how others perceive you.

Yes, you are a fixer. Your overindulgence with other people's lives is a direct result of your feeling that you are unable to fix your own life. The reality is that you are a giving, loving person who empathizes with others. That is not a bad trait to possess. There are many selfish people in the world who could care less about others. What you have to do is find enough love inside to share with you. That's right. Love you! You deserve to be loved, but until you come to terms with this fact, you will always give more than you get.

Stop living someone else's dream. The difference between you and a person who does not enable is that a non-enabler looks at life with confidence. In reality, he has the same issues and problems that you have; however, he has dared to believe that he can make it through any storm. People who refuse to enable are overcomers of obstacles, setbacks, and disappointment. They believe in who they are and fight hard for who they want to become. You don't have to live in their world. Make your own dream and aspirations.

What you tell yourself matters. If you believe you are a failure, you are; if you believe you are ugly, you are; if you believe you won't make it, you won't; if you believe you have to rescue everyone, you will keep trying; if you believe that you need to clean up other people's messes, you will. Get out of your own head with negative thoughts, actions, and behaviors. While you might believe that helping others is a positive action, it actually turns negative when the help hinders the person or stops him or her from taking responsibility for his or her own actions.

The biggest hurdle that I had to overcome regarding my public indictment and imprisonment was shame and guilt. Waking up every day and seeing my picture on the front page of the state's largest newspaper sent me into a state of severe depression. I made a conscious decision not to read what was printed, but I did go online to see if my name appeared. I remember thinking that this was all a dream that would soon end. The dream lingered for a long time, but in the midst of the horror, I rid myself of a powerful adversary by the name of shame. The reality was I had a lot of things which caused me to harbor shame: a drug addict father, I had been molested as a child, living on welfare. But this event in my life was the most visible scar; it filled me with hurt and pain. Every day for what seemed like eternity my heart came through my chest and my head pulsated with a large continuous thump. The shame of the most recent events only aggravated the pre-existing shame which I had carried most of my life.

I removed the persecution complex from my mind, soul, and voice. If you want to win the battle of shame and guilt, first get over you. Yes, get over the idea that you violated a personal code which says you can do no wrong. Remove the thought, "If only I had . . ." When you get the urge to think negative thoughts about yourself, speak life into the atmosphere surrounding you. There is a biblical Scripture, which says, "The power of the tongue is death or life." You have to make a choice between death, a sense of finality in your life and situation, or life, the gift that breathes fresh perspectives into your thoughts and actions. Mistakes are opportunities to learn and grow. Stop harboring bad feelings about the mistakes you have made. Ask for forgiveness from the only true power that matters, which is God. Get up, dust yourself off, and keep moving. There is untapped goodness inside of you. Surrender to your goodness. Don't punish yourself. Let it go!

Fall in love with you! If you have spent years in self-hatred, disappointment, and shame, it is time to release, let go, and let God. Commit to love you, show your loyalty to you. Most enablers act out of selfishness, even if they don't know it. You boost your self-esteem when you recognize the good in you. You are able to love others more freely when you first love yourself freely.

REFLECTION EXERCISE:
CHAPTER NINE

When is the last time that you did something just for you?

_____

_____

_____

While you are spending time alone, do you find yourself constantly thinking about other people's issues - family, children, or friends?

_____

_____

_____

When you are having a difficult time emotionally, do you hide behind a smile and humor?

_____

_____

_____

Are you worried about what other people may think of you? Write a love letter to yourself. In it, describe all of the things you love about you. You might be surprised about what you have to say.

_____

_____

_____

Chapter Ten
WHAT THE SCRIPTURES SAY ABOUT ENABLING

"Live Biblically."
-Dr. Lesly Devereaux

AS DISCUSSED EARLIER in this book you enable if you perpetuate another person's self-destructive behavior. This usually occurs when you protect that person from the painful consequences that could actually serve as a motivation to change. There are several Scriptures which address the issue of enabling by instructing us how we should relate to one another. The main premise which sounds the alarm is that enabling, which is a derivative of codependency patterns, allows people to take precedent over God. Instead of depending on God, the tendency of enablers is to allow a codependent relationship to exist, relying on each other for emotional and sometimes physical needs rather than taking care of themselves.

A glaring contradiction which exists in this type of relationship is that between faith and trust in God, and dependence on individuals. Our faith fuels our relationship with God. When we turn to others to fulfill emotional needs, which can be self-destructive, we are saying in essence that we don't need God, because our strength lies in what we perceive our capabilities or the capabilities of others to be. This pattern of enabling causes there to be a deficiency in the area of self-care. It is important to understand that self-care is not an act of being selfish; rather it is just what it says – care of one's self. Critical to the wholeness of any relationship, even to the welfare of one's being, is the need for self-care.

The question of self-care becomes important and is supported scripturally. The enabler should pause to consider the behavior of Jesus. He was consistent with self-care. From the time that Jesus was a young boy in the temple and separated from his parents, he understood the importance of self-care, declaring to his parents "Why did you seek me? Did you know that I must be about My Father's business?" (Luke 2:49). The encounter is less about the worry of Jesus' parents and more about Jesus' desire to take care of spiritual business which strengthened him. The problem with enablers is that they are about everyone's business but their own to the point of burn out. None of the business that an enabler focuses on helps them or the other person.

Another important example of the habits of Jesus was his disciplined prayer life. The Scriptures declare that after beginning his ministry on earth, he traveled among the people healing the sick and performing miracles. When word got out about the power that Jesus possessed crowds gathered to hear, and to be healed by him, of their infirmities. Consequently, "He Himself often withdrew into the wilderness and prayed." (Luke 5:15-16). Enablers often assume only one part of the Scriptural scenario of Jesus, which is – they try to heal or fix everyone. What is absent is the withdrawal time necessary to care for self. Jesus understood the necessity of self-care for his well-being and was unapologetic when it came to taking care of his own needs.

It is important not to confuse doing good for others as enabling. God wants us to love our neighbors as ourselves and to do good. But when doing good surfaces from a place of need or acting when we really can't or shouldn't, we operate from a place of weakness which is not of God. "All of our strength comes from God who made the heavens and the earth." (Psalm 124:8).

Scripturally it appears that God wants us to form dependence on Him and His power and independence from those who we seek to control. The healthy relationship exists between co-dependents when interdependence is established. That is, individuals in the relationship are mutually dependent on the other. This differs from a dependence relationship, where one person is dependent and the other is not. In an interdependent relationship people may be emotionally, or morally responsible to each other but it is not to the detriment of one. "Not forsaking the assembling of ourselves together, as is the manner of some, but exhorting one another, and so much the more as you see the day approaching." (Hebrews 10:25). Codependents should lift each other up and not tear each other down to the point that the relationship becomes exhausting.

The interdependence journey involves key actions which will help to form healthy relationships: integrity, maturity, change, and commitment; these actions can be found by reading and embracing the Scriptures. Your integrity is compromised each time you make excuses or perpetuate the behavior of the enabled. "Therefore, preparing your minds for action, and being sober-minded, set your hopefully on the grace that will be brought to you at the revelation of Jesus Christ. As obedient children, do not be conformed to the passions of your former ignorance, but as he who called you is holy, you also be holy in your conduct." (1 Peter 1:13-15). God wants us to put away the desires of dishonesty and to walk upright and circumspect. Mature relationships involve seeking God for wisdom when confronted with the challenge of codependency. "If any of you lacks wisdom, let him ask of God, who gives to us liberally and without reproach, and it will be given to him." (James 1:5). Enablers have the tendency to act before they think which in most cases, causes trouble for them and the enabled. Seek God in all that you require because he makes himself available and supplies your needs. Change can be a challenging concept because we tend to operate within our comfort zone. The change needed for the individual seeking to be free from codependency may require a different way of looking at how you see yourself. "As long as my breath is in me, and the breath of God in my nostrils, my lips will not speak wickedness, nor my tongue utter deceit." (Job 27:3-4). The enabler's responsibility is first to be watchful over their own self. You have to face what you fear, which is the misconception of power that is gained by controlling others.

Finally, enablers should make a commitment which involves becoming a new creature. "Therefore, if anyone is in Christ, he is a new creation; old things have passed away; behold, all things have become new." (2 Corinthians 5:17). You have to fight for the new you because there may be many situations which you find yourself in that cause you to fall back into your old self-centered behavior.

Bible Verses Useful for Meditation

GALATIANS 1:10 ESV

"Am I now seeking the approval of man, or of God? Or am I trying to please man? If I were still trying to please man, I would not be a servant of Christ.

GALATIANS 6:1-5 ESV

"Brothers, if a man is caught in any transgression, you who are spiritual bear one another's burdens, and so fulfill the law of Christ. For if anyone thinks he is something, when he is nothing, he deceives himself. But let each one test his own work, and then his reason to boast will be in himself and not in his neighbor. For each will have to bear his own load."

1 THESSALONIANS 2:4 ESV

"But just as we have been approved by God to be entrusted with the gospel, so we speak, not to please man, but to please God who tests our hearts."

ISAIAH 43:18-19 ESV

"Remember not the former things, nor consider the things of old. Behold, I am doing a new thing; now it springs forth, do you not perceive it? I will make a way in the wilderness and rivers in the desert."

2 CORINTHIANS 5:16-21 ESV

"From now on, therefore, we regard no one according to the flesh. Even though we once regarded Christ according to the flesh, we regard him thus no longer. Therefore, if anyone is in Christ, he is a new creation. The old has passed away; behold, the new has come. All this is from God, who through Christ reconciled us to himself and gave us the ministry of reconciliation; that is, in Christ God was reconciling the world to himself, not counting their trespasses against them, and entrusting to us the message of reconciliation. Therefore, we are ambassadors for Christ, God making his appeal through us. We implore you on behalf of Christ, be reconciled to God."

PROVERBS 3:5-6 ESV

"Trust in the Lord with all your heart, and do not lean on your own understanding."

1 PETER 5:7 ESV

"Casting all your anxieties on him, because he cares for you."

GALATIANS 5:1-26 ESV

"For freedom Christ has set us free; stand firm therefore, and do not submit again to a yoke of slavery. Look, I, Paul, say to you that if you accept circumcision, Christ will be of no advantage to you. I testify again to every man who accepts circumcision that he is obligated to keep the whole law. You are severed from Christ, you who would be justified by the law; you have fallen away from grace. For through the Spirit, by faith, we ourselves eagerly wait for the hope of righteousness."

PSALM 118:6 ESV

"The Lord is on my side; I will not fear. What can man do to me?"

JOHN 14:26 ESV

"But the Helper, the Holy Spirit, whom the Father will send in my name, he will teach you all things and bring to your remembrance all that I have said to you."

1 CORINTHIANS 10:33 ESV

"Just as I try to please everyone in everything I do, not seeking my own advantage, but that of many, that they may be saved."

ISAIAH 53:1-12 ESV

"Who has believed what he has heard from us? And to whom has the arm of the Lord been revealed? For he grew up before him like a young plant, and like a root out of dry ground; he had no form or majesty that we should look at him, and no beauty that we should desire him. He was despised and rejected by men; a man of sorrows, and acquainted with grief; and as one from whom men hide their faces he was despised, and we esteemed him not. Surely he has borne our griefs and carried our sorrows; yet we esteemed him stricken, smitten by God, and afflicted. But he was wounded for our transgressions; he was crushed for our iniquities; upon him was the chastisement that brought us peace, and with his stripes we are healed."

GALATIANS 1:15-16 ESV

"But when he who had set me apart before I was born, and who called me by his grace, was pleased to reveal his Son to me, in order that I might preach him among the Gentiles, I did not immediately consult with anyone;"

Psalm 1:3 ESV

"He is like a tree planted by streams of water that yields its fruit in its season and its leaf does not wither. In all that he does, he prospers."

1 John 3:19-20 ESV

"By this we shall know that we are of the truth and reassure our heart before him; for whenever our heart condemns us, God is greater than our heart, and he knows everything."

Acts 15:8 ESV

"And God, who knows the heart, bore witness to them, by giving them the Holy Spirit just as he did to us,"

Luke 16:15 ESV

"And he said to them, "You are those who justify yourselves before men, but God knows your hearts. For what is exalted among men is an abomination in the sight of God.""

Psalm 1:3 ESV

"O Lord, you have searched me and known me! You know when I sit down and when I rise up; you discern my thoughts from afar. You search out my path and my lying down and are acquainted with all my ways. Even before a word is on my tongue, behold, O Lord, you know it altogether. You hem me in, behind and before, and lay your hand upon me."

1 Samuel 16:7 ESV

"But the Lord said to Samuel, "Do not look on his appearance or on the height of his stature, because I have rejected him. For the Lord sees not as man sees: man looks on the outward appearance, but the Lord looks on the heart."

COLOSSIANS 1:1-29 ESV

"Paul, an apostle of Christ Jesus by the will of God, and Timothy our brother, To the saints and faithful brothers in Christ at Colossae: Grace to you and peace from God our Father. We always thank God, the Father of our Lord Jesus Christ, when we pray for you, since we heard of your faith in Christ Jesus and of the love that you have for all the saints, because of the hope laid up for you in heaven. Of this you have heard before in the word of the truth, the gospel,"

ISAIAH 49: 8-9 ESV

"Thus says the Lord: "In a time of favor I have answered you; in a day of salvation I have helped you; I will keep you and give you as a covenant to the people, to establish the land, to apportion the desolate heritages, saying to the prisoners, 'Come out,' to those who are in darkness, 'Appear.' They shall feed along the ways; on all bare heights shall be their pasture;"

REFLECTION EXERCISE:
CHAPTER TEN

The purpose of this exercise is to empower you with words of affirmation each day.

_____

_____

_____

Choose a verse from the list in the chapter and verbalize it each day for 7 days.

_____

_____

_____

Choose another verse that resonates with you; verbalize it each day for 14 days.

_____

_____

_____

Continue through the list until you have worked up to verbalizing a Scripture verse for 21 days. Anything done for 21 days of more can become a habit.

_____

_____

_____

.

Chapter Eleven
THE UPSIDE TO FAILURE

"Tell yourself, "I'm not a failure. I failed at doing something. "There's a big difference."
-Erma Bombeck

KEEP YOUR HEAD ABOVE THE NOISE

IT IS DIFFICULT to imagine that there can be an upside to failure; after all, failure is synonymous with lack of success, inability to perform, neglect, dereliction, oversight or nonfeasance. The blanket fact is that you messed up in some area. Depending on what it is, there may be difficulty in trying to recover or the recovery could take longer than expected. I had to wrestle with this reality. For many years after my debacle I replayed my failure in my mind; If only I had not taken the job in Trenton; if only I had not had the relationships with some people; if only I had not tried to help my sister and mother; if only I had paid closer attention to the politics; and if only I had been a better leader. The regrets were innumerable. Each time I considered a regret I became angry at myself, calling out on several occasions as I looked at my reflection in the mirror, stupid, idiot, selfish and some names I will not mention. After a short stint with the possibility of ending my life, yes suicide, I just wanted the nightmare to be over so that I could move on with my life.

One important consideration that I had to reconcile was the fact that just because I failed did not mean that I was a failure. Admittedly I was on the fence on many occasions. There were times that I did think that I was a failure. This was no small misstep I had committed. It was big and even if I was being used as an example, I opened the door. The thought that crept through my mind was that there had to be something terribly wrong with me in order for me to make such a huge blunder.

A few years into the challenge which lay before me, I began to realize that this was a head issue, meaning I had to stop focusing on the failure and instead dissect the reason for the failure. An important step was learning to keep my head above the noise, the constant stares when I entered a room where my former colleagues may have gathered; the hush when I entered the home of some of my family members during holiday gatherings. The noise was only a distraction which I allowed. As I tried to move away from the negative thoughts I began to metaphorically play beautiful music in my ears which sounded like success. The reason for the failure was that I allowed myself to become vulnerable in areas which had always been perceived as strength. In essence my strength, which was the ability to take control in situations, became my weakness because I was not using my ability in the way that was beneficial to me or others.

Once I understood the reason for my failure I was able to move in such a manner that shielded me from the negative talk. I no longer cared what others said; only with how I responded and what I was doing to correct my wrong so that I could start living again. The overachiever in me refused to allow me to remain stagnant. With a Juris Doctorate in hand, I found myself in seminary working on my Masters of Divinity. I moved on to the Ministerial Institute of my denomination and earned two ordinations, Deacon and Elder, in the African Methodist Episcopal Church. I earned a second Doctorate, this time in ministry, writing my thesis on the very issue in which I believed I had failed, "Leading with Ministry in Mind." This was my way of keeping my head above the noise and moving forward. I became determined to overcome the obstacle instead of allowing the obstacle to consume me. I am convinced that if it had not been for the failures I would never have entered seminary earning a masters and a second doctorate, which I consider great accomplishments.

In order to overcome the propensity to think of yourself as a failure when you fail at something, and you will fail at something, you must refuse to accept the reality of the failure. In spite of the challenge you must persevere by keeping your head up when the great wind of adversity tries to knock you down. You may bend but you do not have to break.

"God uses people who fail because there aren't any other kind around."
-Unknown Author

DON'T DEVALUE YOURSELF

There is the tendency to devalue one's self when personal failure strikes. During the initial years of my problems I fell into the trap. I thought that I was not a very good person in any respect because of what I allowed to transpire. It was difficult for me to maintain a positive mindset. With the honors I received for my work as an attorney to the hundreds of games that I attended as a proud mom supporting my sons, I felt like a failure. Consumed with the thoughts I weighed myself down and for a little while was not able to move forward. I set out on a quest to read the entire Bible, something I had never attempted as a Christian. As I read I began to see a pattern. From Genesis to Revelation the Bible was filled with a cast of flawed characters. Every one that God used to do great work either suffered personal failures or faced major adversity. I began to think that it was possible for me to foster a positive attitude even in failure because I could turn a negative situation into something positive and use it to do good for my family and others.

Psychologist Martin E. Seligman believes that we have two choices when we fail: We can internalize or externalize our failure. "People who fail…think they are worthless, talentless, unlovable. People who blame external events do not lose self-esteem when bad events strike." I had to keep my perspective and realize that taking responsibility for my actions was not synonymous with being a failure. What occurred in my life was what I now consider "a wrinkle in my forehead" or a bend in the road but not the end of the road. Both are temporary and can easily be eradicated. It was up to me not to internalize but realize the mistake that I made, to keep trying and to believe in my potential even when others doubted.

A friend sent a card to me and in her own handwriting simply wrote, "This too shall pass." Admittedly while in the heat of battle all I saw was a deep dark endless hole that was trying to swallow me up. The more I fought to try and regain my footing in life I realized that I could not let this single incident define me. I wrote out the positive and negative qualities that I possessed and realized that there was so much more to me than one isolated incident and no matter what the immediate outcome I would be able to move forward. Focusing on my strengths instead of my failures gave me the opportunity to consider how I could use my strong qualities to bounce back, regain my footing and move forward in my life.

"Failure offers you the chance to turn adversity into opportunity."
-Author, John C. Maxwell

A Bad Situation Turned Good

For the past ten years I have worked extra hard to turn a bad situation into something good. The writing of this book is the culmination of a journey to redemption. While the Christian in me knows and understands that because of the Grace and Mercy of Jesus Christ who died for my sins that I am forgiven, I realized that my failures, trials and struggles could serve a greater purpose. It was important for the experience of the trial, public humiliation and prison not to be in vain. Fighting my way through the pain and negative feelings took time. As already mentioned I furthered my education and I entered the ministry. But I took self-reflective steps as well. Always known for my assertive manner, I began to tone down my presentation. The character traits which were present in my personality I examined and decided whether they helped or hurt me on my journey. Humility was not a word often associated with me but something I wanted to embrace and I did. This was my opportunity to chip away at the character flaws which at times overshadowed the many accomplishments in my life.

John C. Maxwell said it best, "Adversity lies at the heart of every success. The process of achievement comes through repeated failures and the constant struggle to climb to a higher level." This very powerful revelation is what should get you out of the bed and out of your head when you fail. Instead of running away from the failure, embrace and learn from it. I learned so much from my failure and it really is what gave me the energy and desire to reposition myself. When you fall as low as I did the only direction you can go is up. While you may never end up in prison and I hope that you don't, if you are working toward a goal you are open to failure. Use the failure to fuel your mind in such a manner that the only way for you is up.

Before I left for prison in 2008 I formed a nonprofit called Resilience Ministries. Not sure where God was leading me, I knew one day I would use it. In developing a mission statement I defined what resilience means which is to bounce back, to have buoyancy. My intent is to use the ministry to help formally incarcerated women who need emotional support when they return to society. All of the women that I met in prison failed at something in their life or they would not have been there. There were some that would leave prison and never return. There would be others for whom prison was a revolving door. For women like me the key to never returning to prison was our ability to bounce back. I was determined never to return to the belly of the beast that is prison and so I did the work necessary to insure that I would not return. I became a stronger, wiser and a better person because of my adversity and of what I had overcome.

DAVID A MAN OF JOY AND SORROW

The Bible is full of accounts of people dealing with adversity. There was always a choice when dealing with the struggles. Some handled them wisely and some foolishly. David experienced a cycle of joy and sadness. A flawed individual, David's struggles were self-inflicted while others were a part of life. A memorable story is found in 1 Samuel 30. David experienced the pain and anguish of loss. Returning to Ziklag with his men, he found that the Amalekites had made a raid against the Negev and against Ziklag. They had overcome Ziklag and burned it with fire. The Amalekites took all of the women and children captive. When David and his men returned to the city, they found it burned with fire, and their wives and sons and daughters gone. Then David and the men that were with him raised their voices and wept until they had no more strength to weep.

FROM CHIEF SOLDIER TO ACCUSED

Imagine being in a position of leadership with so many people counting on you and then something goes terribly wrong. You have now gone from being the one who people looked to for strength and guidance to one who people blame. This is what happened to David. The people spoke of stoning him, because all the people were hurting to the core for their sons and daughters. David became greatly distressed. With no one around to turn to, David strengthened himself in the Lord. Despite all of the destruction and chaos around him he took an adverse situation and instead of allowing it to consume him he looked for an option which gave him peace and wisdom.

Adversity Turned into Opportunity

David faced a real situation which threatened his life and the lives of his family members. This adversity could have broken him but he persevered. Instead of over-reacting, he took time to seek guidance from God. It started with him asking Abiathar the priest, the son of Ahimelech, to bring him the ephod. Abiathar brought the ephod to David who inquired of the Lord. He asked should he pursue after the enemy and would he overtake them. The Lord told David to pursue because he would surely overtake and rescue his family. David did as the Lord said and took his men to the enemy camp. Catching them off guard, David and his men attacked and reclaimed all that had been taken by the Amalekites. David's adversity presented him with the opportunity to ask God for guidance. There is no problem too big or small for God. It is a wonderful feeling to know that we can go to him with every situation. David's adversity also gave him the chance to wait on God. The scene at Ziklag was devastating. David was under tremendous pressure and his life was in danger. He did not rush to a decision. He waited for God to answer his prayer. When you face the mountains of life that sometime come with defeat, it is good to take time to be still. Don't try to over think your situation. Seek wisdom for the right way to recover. David did just that – he waited for the right answer from God and when he received it, he made his move. Over-thinking failure and adversity has the tendency to cause stress which is not good for you or the people around you. The time spent stressing can be well spent seeking wisdom and knowing the right time to move. David's final action was simply trusting God. It started with him knowing that He could go to God and be heard and then trusting enough to wait for an answer, and finally waiting for God to give him the victory. We can all learn from David as we try to handle the adversities that come with failure. David was able to overcome because he prayed, waited, trusted and strengthened himself in the Lord. If he did it so can we.

"Life is 10% of what happens to you
and 90% of how you react to it."
-Charles R. Swindoll

IT'S NOT THE FALLING DOWN BUT THE GETTING BACK UP THAT MATTERS

I remember driving to the Philadelphia International Airport with my aunt, on my way to see my mother in California. It was 2007 the summer that the trial was set to begin. I said to her that since the inception of my problems I had not had one good night of sleep. I felt like I had fallen into a dark hole and I could not get out of it. She softly said I know it must be hard but I know my niece and you will pick yourself up and get out of the hole.

On the five-hour plane ride to California I thought about what my aunt said. I knew I wanted to get out of the dark pit that I was in. It was going to take much more than my desires or dreams to make it happen. My life was still in limbo because the trial had not started and when it did I had no idea what my fate would be. Reflecting on my seminary experience as a student, I immersed in the study of theology. I had no real destination in terms of minis-try but as I absorbed the Scriptures and stories of hardship, pain, victory and joy that are all prevalent in biblical teaching, my soul quieted. So many people fell but with the hand of God they were able to get back up.

As the days passed, my focus was no longer on my fall but I became driven by the fact that one day I would get back up. How became the question. In October 2008 after ten months in the belly of the beast – prison – I was welcomed home by a courtroom full of family and friends who had showed up in support of my return to society. It was a wonderful day. I was finally physically free from the shackles and humiliation which comes with being an inmate. I ate lunch with my husband and retired to the security of my home. I thought often about how I would make my re-entry into society and suffered a bit of trepidation. However, I overcame my anxiety when I thought about the positive that could come out of my hardship. The reality is that it takes more than just thoughts, persistence or even resilience to get back up after a fall. I possessed all of these traits but I needed to move forward with steps that were based on what I call the "P Factor," Prayer, Purpose, Plan, Preparation, Perseverance, Progress.

PRAYER

Whenever there is an opportunity to tap into the higher power that is God, go for it! When trouble hits it is easy to want to run to other people for reassurance. Surrounding yourself with a community of friends that you can share your joys and sorrows with is not bad. However, there are times when people are not what you need. Prayer offers you the opportunity to focus inward and upward. Resurfacing from failure really is an inside job. As I have said throughout this book you have to work on emotions and distractions. Looking upward to God as you work on the internal baggage provides the strength, guidance and confidence that you need to move forward.

PURPOSE

Failure can have many residual affects if we leave room for negative thoughts to fester. One important factor to consider when getting back up is purpose. I host a weekly internet radio show called Joyful Living for Women. There are guests that share their struggles, joys, hopes and I do as well. I always end the show with "If you find your purpose you will find your joy." Purpose is what gives you the desire to move forward in life. In Rick Warren's book, The Purpose Driven Life, he starts out saying "You are not a mistake." It is what he did not say that resonates with me. You may make mistakes but you are not a mistake. Once you discover the gifts and talents that you possess and how to use them for your benefit and the benefit of others, joy is yours.

PLAN

It is important to develop a plan as you rise from a fall. First you have to know what you are planning for. You have to aim for something which will bring you results. I aimed for developing a writing and speaking platform which focused on encouraging personal development in women. After failure your goal might be to start your own business or to get out of debt. The important point is that your aspiration provides structure for your plan. No plan is worth the thought given to it without action. So when you are thinking about ways to recover from adversity remember to move forward with the steps that will help you bring the result necessary for success.

PREPARATION

I begin like so many others with a very old saying coined by Benjamin Franklin, "By failing to prepare you are preparing to fail." You must see the opportunity to prepare for the next stage of your life after failure. I prepared myself spiritually by going to seminary; I prepared myself professionally by earning a Master of Divinity and Doctorate of Ministry Degree; I prepared myself for the writing of this book by understanding what I did not know about codependency as it related to my life and others. Whatever it is that you are aiming for you must prepare to reach the goal. You may not always accomplish what you set out to do but as another saying goes, "there is nothing beat by a failure but a try."

PROGRESS

The learning experience which comes from failure is important to understand. Embrace the idea of learning from your mistakes. Self-examination is a first step. Resist the desire to blame other people. As you navigate toward total restoration don't forget to check out your progress. Have you changed behaviors or habits which were instrumental in your failure? Are you moving toward your intended goal? I am constantly reflecting on what I can do better as it relates to my work, character and service for others. Checking out my progress helps to keep me focused on what is important. I can't change the past and neither can you but we can insure that we don't waste our future.

Perseverance

The most challenging of the P Factor is the determination it takes to get back up after failure. Sometimes you fall so low that the very thought of the work necessary to stand on solid ground again is draining. But you must keep trying. My fall from grace was extremely low because my family, finances, career, reputation and relationships were all affected; but if I can get back up so can you. Your attitude will either make you or break you. Stop with the pity party because it won't get you anywhere. It is a matter of emotional survival that you push through the pain, disappointment and disillusionment. With a resolute mind you will get to the other side of failure.

As I closed the challenging chapters of my life I shut out pain, hurt, lack of forgiveness and shame. The upside of my story is filled with joy as I turn the pages of the new chapters in my life. I am happier now than when I practiced law, sat as a judge, and certainly as I moved further away from the bad memories of New Jersey Commerce. I have learned so much as a result of this experience. Being in church most of my life I have heard many expressions of wisdom from senior members. As I reflect on the good and bad days between 2004 and 2008, I hear my Grandmother Victoria's voice saying "I won't take nothing for my journey."

Lives Restored: Candace and My Mother

Candace soars! You heard so much about our family struggles and I did not want to leave you with the impression that this is the end of the story. I am happy to report that my sister Candace is doing extremely well. After her two-week stay in MCCC she returned to California and was reunited with our mom and her children. Candace found employment and eventually moved into her own home. She is a regional trainer for an organization and on the weekend she operates a mobile spa business and sells handmade bath and body products at various events. Her product is her own creation and can be found at www.robertimari.biz. She is a loving mother who is busy with church activities. The best news is that Candace stays away from toxic relationships. I am proud to call her sister.

Mommy is a phenomenal woman! As I continue to say, my mom has been a constant in our lives. With everything she has endured in her life and handled with grace and strength I call her phenomenal. Over thirty years ago mommy left New Jersey to begin a new life in California. She hit the ground running. She has mentored hundreds of youth with educational and artistic pursuits. She is very active in her church, and since 2004 when our troubles began, my mom has been honored over a dozen times for her work in the community and with youth. I am grateful that people who really know her dismissed what they heard and focused on the woman they knew and admired. I am proud to call you mommy.

The end of this life chapter brings a new beginning for me! What about you?

REFLECTION EXERCISE:
CHAPTER ELEVEN

If you have a goal that you wish to attain what is it?

_____

_____

_____

What steps do you need to take to obtain your goals?

_____

_____

_____

What is the first thing you need to do to get started?

_____

_____

_____

What obstacles might be in your way of achieving your goals?

_____

_____

_____

Take out a piece of paper and write down one goal. Then list each
step you plan to take to achieve your goals. Find a safe place in your
home or office where you can see the list daily. As you accomplish a
step which moves you closer to achieving your goal, mark it off and
write, Mission Accomplished!

_____

_____

_____

TAKE THE THE ENABLER TEST

This self-assessment will give you a basic understanding about enabling. Look over the list of statements. Indicate in the appropriate box, with a checkmark, how often the statement applies to you: *never or very rarely, sometimes, a good part of the time,* or *most or all of the time.* In assessing the statements, consider each question as applying to the past six months or more.

Statement	Never or very rarely	Sometimes	A good part of the time	Most or all of the time
1. I have a need to rescue people from their situations.				
2. I disregard clear relational boundaries.				
3. I find myself being an excessive accommodator.				
4. I blame myself for the behavior of others.				
5. I am irritated more than people think.				
6. Basic assumptions I have about life have been shattered.				
7. I experience trauma symptoms similar to those experienced by the people I support.				
8. I feel more isolated than usual.				
9. I feel guilty that I can't do more to help.				
10. I have nightmares based on my work experiences and/or the stories shared with me.				

INTERPRETATION: Count up the number of checkmarks you have in two columns: "A good part of the time" and "Most or all of the time." If you have at least three or more checkmarks placed in "A good part of the time" and three or more checkmarks placed in "Most or all of the time," you may be at a greater risk of being an enabler.

This test is not meant to scare you. It is meant to make you aware of the way enablers act and think. Monitor your relational behavior with others for a few months to see if you have a problem yet to be identified.

Adpated from ©2014 Barbara Rubel. Compassion Fatigue Self-Assesment

Epilogue
THE LIFTER OF MY HEAD

"For he will hide me in his shelter in the day of trouble;
he will conceal me under cover of his tent; he will lift me
high upon a rock. And now my head shall be lifted up..."
-Psalm 27:5-6

I HAVE BEEN WRITING THIS BOOK FOR THE PAST TEN YEARS. IT HAS BEEN a long journey to find my voice, one that healed me and helped others. It was in 2004 that I was asked to resign from my position as Chief of staff. My boss told me that I may need to get a lawyer. In all honesty when he uttered the words it did not register. I replied, "A lawyer for what?" Although not practicing law at the time in my naive moment I did not grasp why on earth I would need legal representation. My boss did not have an answer he just passed a message from the chief of staff in the governor's office regarding my situation. I remained in denial regarding the suggestion until I started receiving phone calls from the press as well as calls from former colleagues who wanted to know if what had surfaced about my conduct was in fact true.

The light bulb finally went off in my head and I sought legal representation. Each day the allegations intensified. Finally, on a day that remains a fog my face hit the front page of the state's largest newspaper. I never saw the article I just heard about it from friends and frenemies. (People who pretend to be your friend but really are not). After the newspaper came the television news report. My world quickly began to unravel as I watched my reputation, go from smart, competent and professional to misguided, troubled and criminal.

My heart palpitated and my head sunk low. I retreated to the sitting area which is off from my bedroom. Parking my body on the couch I lay in a tight fetal position for weeks, unable to lift my head from the pillow. My husband would call home from work to check on me while my youngest son was in school. I could barely talk to him and I refused to speak with anyone else. He said, "Lesly you have to get off of the couch." I responded "I can't."

The years following the initial revelations were tough and as you have read in this book I suffered major consequences for the error of my ways. It has been ten years since the horrible revelation that I was in deep mess. Opportunities have come my way and I have worked hard to redeem myself.

Many people abandoned ship during my troubles. People that I either considered friends or close colleagues stopped talking to me. Fast forward to 2014, I get joy when I think about what the Lord is doing in my life. Some of the most moving moments for me are when people, especially women approach and say that they admire me because I have overcome a major obstacle and still have a smile on my face. I smile because I understand that I could not have made it without God on my side.

I recently attended an affair which honored a close friend. When she called to invite me initially I hesitated because it was a gathering of some of my former colleagues in the legal profession. Paulette was a true friend who never wavered in her support during my ordeal. I decided to put aside my insecurity and attend the event. When I walked into the hotel I was greeted with hugs, kisses and tears by people who were genuinely happy to see me. It was a wonderful evening and I was happy that I decided to attend. A few days later I traveled to Maryland to spend a few days with my son Jaison. One morning as I took my daily walk around the nearby school track I reflected on the past ten years. I had fallen as low as one could go financially, professionally and emotionally. I thought to myself, "girl with all the stuff you have been through it is a miracle that you are still here." I continued with the thought, how could

I find the strength to resurface, the courage to re-enter society, the confidence to stand in a pulpit and preach God's Word, the tenacity to start my own radio show, speaking and coaching business, and to write a book telling many of my secrets?

I felt a wonderful movement on my inside and a still small voice in my ear. It was God saying, "Lesly I am the lifter of your head." To God I say, THANK YOU!

About the Author

REV. DR. LESLY R. DEVEREAUX, D.MIN., J.D.

DR. LESLY DEVEREAUX is a graduate of Rutgers University with a Bachelor of Arts degree. She earned her Juris Doctorate from Howard University School of Law and practiced law for more than 15 years. She has traveled extensively throughout the United States and abroad in her professional capacity, counseling individuals as well as business and religious entities in areas of business start-up and development. As a corporate executive, she traveled globally (Ghana, South Africa, China, Greece, Korea, Japan, Bulgaria, Barbados), matching U.S. small business owners with small business owners in other countries for joint venture opportunities.

With an irresistible desire to serve the Lord, she entered New Brunswick Theological Seminary in 2005 where she earned a Masters of Divinity degree, Summa Cum Laude. While in seminary, she became the first African American and first woman to hold the position of Class President. In 2013 she received her Doctor of Ministry degree. Her published thesis is "Leading with Ministry in Mind: Empowering Church Leaders to Move From Task to Ministry Through Spiritual Discernment."

Dr. Devereaux has an abiding commitment to the church and community relating with ease to both venues and using her influence to mentor individuals seeking to gain a closer relationship with God. She preaches and facilitates workshops in a variety of venues. Dr. Devereaux also has an additional publication written to inspire and encourage others who have faced challenges in their life. On This Day Remember: What God Does Not Want You to Forget, A Woman's Daily One-Minute Devotional.

A sought after speaker and mentor in the area of personal development and business, Dr. Devereaux is also the founder and CEO of Joyful Living for Women and the host of the weekly talk show Joyful Living for Women Talk Radio, (located on Blog talk radio).

Joyful Living for Women was launched because Dr. Devereaux wants individuals to know that even in tough situations there are no limitations other than the ones allowed to take residence in the mind.

Through her radio show, articles, seminars, and keynotes, Dr. Devereaux provides resources that encourage individuals to foster positive thinking to dictate their emotions and behavior.

Dr. Devereaux believes in total transparency and readily admits to experiencing successes and failures in business and in life. She believes that both her triumphs and challenges make her uniquely qualified to assist in transforming the lives of women.

Dr. Lesly Devereaux is available to speak at your next conference, workshop, retreat or mastermind. Please visit her website at www.leslydevereaux.com or email drdevereauxL@gmail.com

You can also connect with her via social media at: facebook.com/joyfullivingforwomen; @leslydevereaux on Twitter; LinkedIn or Pintrest.

APPENDIX A

Here are additional questions that are characteristic of the behavior of an enabler.

DO YOU:

- [ ] Have insecurity about self-worth?
- [ ] Feel responsible for the behavior of others close to you?
- [ ] Excuse the bad behavior of others?
- [ ] Have an addiction to helping someone who exhibits bad behavior?
- [ ] Feel worthless unless you are helping others?
- [ ] Have a Messiah complex believing only you can help?
- [ ] Have a need to feel important?
- [ ] Feel rejected if someone says they don't need your help?
- [ ] Measure your self-esteem by what you do for others?
- [ ] Constantly offer advice when not requested?
- [ ] Complain about other bad behavior but feel you must help them anyway?
- [ ] Feel that the drug addict, abuser, gambler, or excessive spender you know can't make it without you?

Note: From breaking Codependency (2015), Devereaux, L.

EXTENDED SELF-DETACHMENT EXERCISE

This exercise it meant to be done over a course of a week. When you write your thoughts on paper and walk away for a while, upon return, in many instances, you will see these differently and are more willing to take the steps necessary to change.

Take out a piece of paper and a pen. Sit down in a quiet space without distractions. Draw a straight line down the middle of the paper. At the top of the paper on one side, put the word LIKE. On the other side, put the word DIS-LIKE. Now, remember self-detachment deals with removal of traits that are causing you harm. The first step in figuring this out is being honest about what you like and dislike about YOURSELF, not your situation.

Be reflective and honest. We all have things we could or should change. This is a time to pour out everything you can think of, and it does not have to be related to the person you might be enabling. You have a list of what you like and dislike about yourself. If your list involves a person who you may be enabling, take another piece of paper and write a letter to the person reflected in your list. Tell that person what you see and what your opinion is about her or him. This should be done in third person as if you were writing a letter to someone else. Seal the letter in an envelope; put a stamp on it; and mail it to yourself. In a few days, when you receive the letter in the mail, open and read it as if it came from someone else who is telling you about yourself.

Write down how reading the letter makes you feel. Decide if there are things you agree with in terms of change in your attitude and actions and begin the slow process of first self-detaching and then detaching those things from your life.

APPENDIX B

THE TWELVE STEPS OF VARIOUS ORGANIZATIONS

ALCOHOLICS ANONYMOUS

1. We admitted we were powerless over alcohol-that our lives had become unmanageable.
2. Came to believe that a Power greater than ourselves could restore us to sanity.
3. Made a decision to turn our will and our lives over to the care of God as we understood Him.
4. Made a searching and fearless moral inventory of ourselves.
5. Admitted to God, to ourselves, and to another human being the exact nature of our wrongs.
6. Were entirely ready to have God remove all these defects of character.
7. Humbly asked Him to remove our shortcomings.
8. Made a list of all persons we had harmed, and became willing to make amends to them all.
9. Made direct amends to such people wherever possible, except when to do so would injure them or others.
10. Continued to take personal inventory and when we were wrong promptly admitted it.
11. Sought through prayer and meditation to improve our conscious contact with God, as we understood Him, praying only for knowledge of His will for us and the power to carry that out.
12. Having had a spiritual awakening as the result of these steps, we tried to carry this message to alcoholics, and to practice these principles in all our affairs.

CO-DEPENDENTS ANONYMOUS (CODA)

1. We admitted we were powerless over others-that our lives had become unmanageable.
2. Came to believe that a Power greater than ourselves could restore us to sanity
3. Made a decision to turn our will and our lives over to the care of God as we understood God.
4. Made a searching and fearless moral inventory of ourselves.
5. Admitted to God, to ourselves, and to another human being the exact nature of our wrongs.
6. Were entirely ready to have God remove all these defects of character.
7. Humbly asked God to remove our shortcomings.
8. Made a list of all persons we had harmed and became willing to make amends to them all.
9. Made direct amends to such people wherever possible, except when to do so would injure them or others.
10. Continued to take personal inventory and when we were wrong, promptly admitted it.
11. Sought through prayer and meditation to improve our conscious contact with God as we understood God, praying only for knowledge of God's will for us and the power to carry that out.
12. Having had a spiritual awakening as the result of these steps, we tried to carry this message to other co-dependents, and to practice these principles in all our affairs.

1. We admitted we were powerless over alcohol-that our lives had become unmanageable.
2. Came to believe that a Power greater than ourselves could restore us to sanity
3. Made a decision to turn our will and our lives over to the care of God as we understood Him.
4. Made a searching and fearless moral inventory of ourselves.
5. Admitted to God, to ourselves, and to another human being the exact nature of our wrongs.
6. Were entirely ready to have God remove all these defects of character.
7. Humbly asked Him to remove our shortcomings.
8. Made a list of all persons we had harmed, and became willing to make amends to them all.
9. Made direct amends to such people wherever possible, except when to do so would injure them or others.
10. Continued to take personal inventory and when we were wrong promptly admitted it.
11. Sought through prayer and meditation to improve our conscious contact with God as we understood Him, praying only for knowledge of His will for us and the power to carry that out.
12. Having had a spiritual awakening as the result of these steps, we tried to carry this message to others, and to practice these principles in all our affairs.

GAM-ANON

1. We admitted we were powerless over the problem in our family.
2. Came to believe that a power greater than ourselves could restore us to a normal way of thinking and living. Gam-Anon states that a belief in a Higher Power along with an honest look at themselves will help to resolve their fears, worries, and suspicions.
3. Made a decision to turn our will and our lives over to the care of this power of our own understanding. Step three is the willingness to accept the will of a Higher Power and to let go of self-will. Self-will is said to be at the very root of bitterness, worries, and unhappiness among Gam-Anon members.
4. Made a searching and fearless moral inventory of ourselves. This can be a very difficult step since most Gam-Anon members have been blaming the gambler for his or her own shortcomings. Gam-Anon provides a list of personal assets and liabilities to use as a guideline when working on step four.
5. Admitted to ourselves and to another human being the exact nature of our wrongs. In this step one seeks out a person who can be trusted to share the information from his or her fourth step inventory. As the person "unloads" his or her past, a feeling of freedom and peace of mind enables him or her to continue growing in recovery.
6. Were entirely ready to have these defects of character removed. Recognizing and owning personal character defects in steps four and five now allow members to bring about positive change. Gam-Anon states that many of their members begin working on self-pity and resentment toward their long-term goal, which is peace of mind.
7. Humbly ask God (of our understanding) to remove our shortcomings. After becoming well aware of one's short-comings, help is now required in order to change. Having made a decision to turn one's will over to a Higher Power

in step three, it is time to humbly ask Him to remove one's shortcomings.

8. Made a list of all persons we had harmed and became willing to make amends to them all. Step eight asks for a list to be made of all those harmed. Early on it can be difficult to realize how one has harmed so many people. Harsh punishment, misdirected anger and criticizing others can be common reasons for harming family, friends, or co-workers.

9. Made direct amends to such people whenever possible except when to do so would injure them or others. Making amends to those harmed is an opportunity to bring about change in the spirit of love, kindness, and general well-being. Step nine also states that one should be careful not to hurt anyone in the process of making amends.

10. Continued to take personal inventory and when we were wrong, promptly admitted it. Complacency can lead back to old feelings and behaviors. Step ten asks to reflect on oneself on a daily basis to evaluate one's own progress or shortcomings. Step ten also requires the person to admit to any wrongdoing immediately Following this step will lead toward spiritual growth and serenity

11. Sought through prayer and meditation to improve our conscious contact with God, as we understood Him, praying only for knowledge of His will for us, and the power to carry that out. This step will open the door to a new and more spiritual way of living. It is suggested to start each day with a prayer or thought of one's Higher Power to make each day a better day

12. Having made an effort to practice these principles in all our affairs, we tried to carry this message to others. Having had some measure of success in working through the other steps, it is now time to carry out the main purpose of the Gam-Anon program, which is to help others who are still suffering from the gambling problem in their home.

NAR-ANON

1. We admitted we were powerless over the addict-that our lives have become unmanageable.
2. Came to believe that a Power greater than ourselves could restore us to sanity.
3. Made a decision to turn our will and our lives over to the care of God as we understood Him.
4. Made a searching and fearless moral inventory of ourselves.
5. Admitted to God, to ourselves, and to another human being the exact nature of our wrongs.
6. Were entirely ready to have God remove all these defects of character.
7. Humbly asked Him to remove our shortcomings.
8. Made a list of all persons we had harmed, and became willing to make amends to them all.
9. Made direct amends to such people whenever possible except when to do so would injure them or others.
10. Continued to take personal inventory and when we were wrong promptly admitted it.
11. Sought through prayer and meditation to improve our conscious contact with God as we understood Him, praying only for knowledge of His will for us and the power to carry that out.
12. Having had a spiritual awakening as a result of these steps, we tried to carry this message to others, and to practice these principles in all our affairs.

CO-DEPENDENTS OF SEX ADDICTS (COSA)

1. We admitted we were powerless over compulsive sexual behavior-that our lives had become unmanageable.
2. Came to believe that a Power greater than ourselves could restore us to sanity.
3. Made a decision to turn our will and our lives over to the care of God as we understood God.
4. Made a searching and fearless moral inventory of ourselves.
5. Admitted to God, to ourselves, and to another human being the exact nature of our wrongs.
6. Were entirely ready to have God remove all these defects of character.
7. Humbly asked God to remove our shortcomings.
8. Made a list of all persons we had harmed, and became willing to make amends to them all.
9. Made direct amends to such people wherever possible, except when to do so would injure them or others.
10. Continued to take personal inventory and when we were wrong promptly admitted it.
11. Sought through prayer and meditation to improve our conscious contact with God as we understood God, praying only for knowledge of God's will for us and the power to carry that out.
12. Having had a spiritual awakening as the result of these steps, we tried to carry this message to others, and to practice these principles in all areas of our lives.

Resources

**Al-Anon/Alateen Family Group
Headquarters**
1600 Corporate Landing Parkway
Virginia, Beach VA 23454-5617
888-4AL-ANON (888) 425-5617
www.al-anon.alatee.org
wsa@al-anon.org

**Co-Dependents Anonymous
(CoDA) Fellowship Services
Office**
P.O. Box 33577
Phoenix, AZ 85867-3577
602-277-7991
888-444-2359
www.coda.org
outreach@coda.org

**Gam-Anon International
Service Office, Inc.**
P.O. Box 157
Whitestone, NY 11357
718-352-1671
www.gam-anon.org
gamanonoffice@aol.com

**International Service Organization
of Codependents
Of Sex Addicts (or ISO of COSA)**
P.O. Box 14537
Minneapolis, MN 55414
763-537-6904
www.cosa-recovery.org
info@cosa-recovery.org

**Nar-Anon Family Group
Headquarters, Inc.**
22527 Crenshaw Blvd., Suite 200B
Torrance, CA 0505
800-477-6291
310-534-8188
www.nar-anon.org
naranonWSO@gmail.com

BIBLIOGRAPHY

Al-Anon. Twelve Steps and Twelve Traditions. New York: Al-Anon Family Group Headquarters, Inc., 1987.

Beattie, Melody. Codependent No More: Stop controlling Others and Start Caring for Yourself. Center City, Minnesota: Hazelden Publishing and Educational Services, 2001.

Hough, John and Hardy Marshall. Against the Wall: Men's Reality in a Codependent Culture. Center City, Minnesota: Hazelden Publishing and Educational Services, 1991.

Maxwell, John C. Failing Forward: Turning Mistakes into Stepping Stones for Success. Nashville: Thomas Nelson Publishers, 2000.

Maxwell, John C. Today Matters: 12 Daily Practices to Guarantee Tomorrow's Success. Nashville: Thomas Nelson Publishers, 2004.

Mellody, Pia. Facing Codependency: What it is, Where it Comes from, How it Sabotages our Lives. New York: HarperOne Publishers, 2003.

Miller, Angelyn: The Enabler; When helping hurts the ones you love. Tucson, Arizona: Wheatmark Publisher, 2008.

ACADEMIC ARTICLE:

Fuller, Julie A., Warner, Rebecca M. (2000) Family Stressors as Predictors of Codependency. Genetic, Social & General Psychology Monographs. Vol. 126 Issue 1, p.11. m: Lesly Devereaux <drdevereauxl@gmail.com